Songs *of* Ourselves

Volume 2

CAMBRIDGE
International Examinations

CAMBRIDGE
UNIVERSITY PRESS

4843/24, 2nd Floor, Ansari Road, Daryaganj, Delhi-110002

Cambridge University Press is part of the University of Cambridge.

It furthers the University's mission by disseminating knowledge in the pursuit of education, learning and research at the highest international levels of excellence.

www.cambridge.org
Information on this title: www.cambridge.org/9781107447790

First published 2014
Reprinted 2015 , 2016

Printed in India by Shree Maitrey Printech Pvt. Ltd., Noida

A catalogue record for this publication is available from the British Library

ISBN 978-1-107-44779-0 Paperback

Additional resources for this publication at www.cambridgeindia.org

Contents

PART 2

Birds, Beasts, and the Weather

PART 3

Travel, Migration, and Society

PART 4

Love, Wisdom, and Age

PART 5

War, Sleep, and Death

x   Contents

Introduction

This second volume of *Songs of Ourselves* complements *Songs of Ourselves Volume 1.* Cambridge will continue to use both volumes to set poems for study for IGCSE, O level and AS/AL papers in years to come.

Together the two volumes offer a broad selection of poetry in many different forms and styles and on many different subjects, from countries all over the world and by poets from many different backgrounds.

Poems in *Songs of Ourselves Volume 2* come from New Zealand, India, Canada, Singapore, Pakistan, the UK, the USA, and Zimbabwe, and range from the sixteenth century to the twenty-first. There is once again a mixture of the familiar and canonical with more unusual and newer choices, demonstrating how alive the art of writing poetry is around the globe. As with *Songs 1*, this book is meant to whet the appetite for more poetry – and there is plenty more for readers to find.

Each poem can be read on its own, but as it can be entertaining and instructive to look for links and connections, the poems have been arranged in broad thematic groups. Comparing two poems written about a similar theme is a very good way of focusing on what it is that makes each poem unique and how each poem creates its own effects.

The skill of reading closely – thinking about the precise meaning, interpreting through sensitivity to the ways in which language works, and learning to talk and write about this – brings the poems alive for each reader and is also immensely useful in study, work and life.

Often a poem can be interpreted in quite different ways, but provided it is supported by evidence from the text, each reading has its own value: there are no simple 'correct' answers. In order to get inside the world of a poem, it is important to start by reading it carefully at least two or three times. *Everything* is of some significance: so pay attention to every word and the ways in which those words are put together on the page. It is also valuable to read a poem aloud, to gain a fuller appreciation of features such as rhythm and rhyme – the *sound* of the verse.

Learning a poem by heart makes it one's own, and the words will stay in the mind for many years. Sometimes a particular action will become linked to a poem so that the words arise automatically like an old friend. So looking up on a starry night the words are there: *"Bright star, would I were steadfast as thou art..."*

A note on glosses to the poems

Short glosses have been provided where the meaning of words, phrases or names (such as mythological characters) might not be known.

It is assumed that readers will have access to and use a good dictionary, so only the more obviously obscure words have been glossed. The glosses provided could certainly be added to or reworded because that is the nature of poetry: one definition of poetry is that it is *untranslatable* writing.

Glosses should not be taken to indicate that glossed words have particular significance and the glosses do not attempt to explain the poem. They have been deliberately kept to the minimum so that they do not distract from the experience of reading the poem. It is important that students do not feel put off by not knowing every word of a poem on first reading; students should be encouraged by the thought that the most sophisticated reader will often hesitate and wonder about a meaning, and the poet might want us to do just that.

Acknowledgements

Thanks to Noel Cassidy, Russell Carey, and Nick de Somogyi for their help in the making of this anthology.

Mary Wilmer
Cambridge International Examinations

Acknowledgements

"Passion" by Kathleen Raine from *The Collected Poems of Kathleen Raine* (ISBN: 9780903880817), reproduced with permission from Golgonooza Press.

"The Wedding" by Moniza Alvi, *Split World: Poems 1990–2005* (Bloodaxe Books, 2008).

"Tiger in the Menagerie" from *The Striped World* © Emma Jones and reprinted by permission of Faber and Faber Ltd.

"lion heart" by Amanda Chong from *Poems Singapore and Beyond*, reproduced with permission from Ethos Books.

"Heart and Mind" from *Collected Poems* by Edith Sitwell reprinted by permission of Peters Fraser & Dunlop (www.petersfraserdunlop.com) on behalf of the Estate of Edith Sitwell.

"The Uncles" by John Goodby from *A True Prize*, reproduced with permission from Cinnamon Press.

"Surplus Value" by David C. Ward from *Internal Difference*, reproduced with permission from Carcanet Press Limited, 2011.

"In the Park" by Gwen Harwood from *Selected Poems*, reproduced with permission from Penguin Group (Australia), 2001.

"The Lost Woman..." by Patricia Beer from *Collected Poems*, reproduced with permission from Carcanet Press Limited, 1990.

"Stabat Mater" by Sam Hunt from *Collected Poems, Penguin 1980*, permission for use granted by the author.

"Sons, Departing" by John Cassidy from *Night Cries*, Bloodaxe 1982.

"In Praise of Creation" by Elizabeth Jennings from *Collected Poems*, reproduced with permission from Carcanet Press Limited, 1987.

"Blessed by the Indifference..." by Christopher Reid from *The Flowers of Crete*, reproduced with permission from Areté Books.

Judith Wright: "Australia 1970" from *A Human Pattern: Selected Poems* (ETT Imprint, Sydney 2010).

"Coming" by Philip Larkin from *The Complete Poems*, reproduced with permission from Faber and Faber Ltd.

"Stormcock in Elder" by Ruth Pitter, from *Collected Poems* (Enitharmon Press, 1996).

"Eel Tail" by Alice Oswald, permission for use granted by the author.

"Afternoon with Irish Cows" from *Picnic, Lightning*, by Billy Collins, © 1998. Reprinted by permission of the University of Pittsburgh Press.

"You will Know When You Get There" by Allen Curnow from *You Will Know When You Get There: Poems 1979–81*, reproduced with permission from Auckland University Press and copyright holder Tim Curnow.

"The Stars Go Over the Lonely Ocean" by Robinson Jeffers from *Selected Poems*, reproduced with permission from Carcanet Press Limited, 1987.

"At the Bus Station", First published by 'amaBooks, Zimbabwe, 2011' in the collection *Together*, by Julius Chingono and John Eppel.

"The Enemies" by Elizabeth Jennings from *Collected Poems*, reproduced with permission from Carcanet Press Limited, 1987.

"At the "Capitol"" by Kevin Halligan, from *Utopia* (Cambridge, UK: Springfield Books), 2009.

"an afternoon nap" by Arthur Yap, reproduced with permission from Jenny Yap and the Literary Estate of Arthur Yap.

"Shirt" by Robert Pinsky from *Figured Wheel*, reproduced with permission from Carcanet Press Limited, 1996.

"To a Millionaire" by A.R.D. Fairburn from *Selected Poems 1995*, reproduced with permission from A.R.D. Fairburn Literary Estate.

"Song" by George Szirtes, *New and Collected Poems* (Bloodaxe Books, 2008).

"Waterfall" by Lauris Edmond from *Selected Poems*, Bridget Williams Books New Zealand 2001, reproduced with permission from the Literary Estate of Lauris Edmond.

"Rhyme of the Dead Self" by A.R.D. Fairburn, reproduced with permission from A.R.D. Fairburn Literary Estate.

"Nearing Forty" by Derek Walcott from *Collected Poems*, reproduced with permission from Faber and Faber Ltd.

"Distant Fields/ANZAC Parade" by Rhian Gallagher from *Shift*, reproduced with permission from Auckland University Press and Rhian Gallagher.

"Futility" is reproduced from *Wilfred Owen: The War Poems* (Chatto & Windus, 1994), edited by Jon Stallworthy.

Part 1

Love and Family

1

The Clod and the Pebble

WILLIAM BLAKE

'Love seeketh not itself to please,
Nor for itself hath any care,
But for another gives its ease,
And builds a Heaven in Hell's despair.'

So sung a little Clod of Clay
Trodden with the cattle's feet,
But a Pebble of the brook
Warbled out these metres meet:

'Love seeketh only self to please,
To bind another to its delight,
Joys in another's loss of ease,
And builds a Hell in Heaven's despite.'

Clod] lump of clay or earth
metres meet] appropriate rhymes
in . . . despite] in scornful contempt of

2

Song

LADY MARY WROTH

Love a child is ever crying;
   Please him, and he straight is flying;
   Give him he the more is craving,
   Never satisfied with having.

His desires have no measure;
   Endless folly is his treasure;
   What he promiseth he breaketh.
   Trust not one word that he speaketh.

He vows nothing but false matter,
   And to cozen you he'll flatter.
   Let him gain the hand, he'll leave you,
   And still glory to deceive you.

He will triumph in your wailing,
   And yet cause be of your failing.
   These his virtues are, and slighter
   Are his gifts, his favours lighter.

Feathers are as firm in staying,
   Wolves no fiercer in their preying.
   As a child then leave him crying,
   Nor seek him so given to flying.

straight] immediately
false matter] i.e. lies
cozen] deceive
Let him gain the hand] i.e. if you allow him
   to get the upper hand

glory to] relish the opportunity to
his favours lighter] his kindnesses even flimsier
as firm in staying] as rigidly fixed (i.e. not at all)

3

A *Silent* Love

EDWARD DYER

The lowest trees have tops, the ant her gall,
The fly her spleen, the little spark his heat;
The slender hairs cast shadows, though but small,
And bees have stings, although they be not great;
  Seas have their source, and so have shallow springs;
  And love is love, in beggars and in kings.

Where waters smoothest run, there deepest are the fords,
The dial stirs, yet none perceives it move;
The firmest faith is found in fewest words,
The turtles do not sing, and yet they love;
  True hearts have ears and eyes, no tongues to speak;
  They hear and see, and sigh, and then they break.

the ant her gall . . . fly her spleen] i.e. even such tiny creatures possess the means to take offence
  or experience sadness
fords] crossing-points in a river
dial] sun-dial (which tells the time by the gradual change of the sun's shadow)
turtles] doves (mute birds that were supposed to mate for life)

4

Passion

KATHLEEN RAINE

Full of desire I lay, the sky wounding me,
Each cloud a ship without me sailing, each tree
Possessing what my soul lacked, tranquillity.

Waiting for the longed-for voice to speak
Through the mute telephone, my body grew weak
With the well-known and mortal death, heartbreak.

The language I knew best, my human speech
Forsook my fingers, and out of reach
Were Homer's ghosts, the savage conches of the beach.

Then the sky spoke to me in language clear,
Familiar as the heart, than love more near.
The sky said to my soul, 'You have what you desire.

'Know now that you are born along with these
Clouds, winds, and stars, and ever-moving seas
And forest dwellers. This your nature is.

Lift up your heart again without fear,
Sleep in the tomb, or breathe the living air,
This world you with the flower and with the tiger share.'

Then I saw every visible substance turn
Into immortal, every cell new born
Burned with the holy fire of passion.

This world I saw as on her judgment day
When the war ends, and the sky rolls away,
And all is light, love and eternity.

5

Winter Song

ELIZABETH TOLLET

Ask me no more, my truth to prove,
What I would suffer for my love.
With thee I would in exile go
To regions of eternal snow,
O'er floods by solid ice confined,
Through forest bare with northern wind:
While all around my eyes I cast,
Where all is wild and all is waste.
If there the tim'rous stag you chase,
Or rouse to fight a fiercer race,
Undaunted I thy arms would bear,
And give thy hand the hunter's spear.
When the low sun withdraws his light,
And menaces an half-year's night,
The conscious moon and stars above
Shall guide me with my wand'ring love.
Beneath the mountain's hollow brow,
Or in its rocky cells below,
Thy rural feast I would provide,
Nor envy palaces their pride.
The softest moss should dress thy bed,
With savage spoils about thee spread:
While faithful love the watch should keep,
To banish danger from thy sleep.

savage spoils] i.e. the trophies of the hunt

6

Last Sonnet

JOHN KEATS

Bright star, would I were steadfast as thou art—
   Not in lone splendour hung aloft the night,
And watching, with eternal lids apart,
   Like Nature's patient sleepless Eremite,
The moving waters at their priest-like task
   Of pure ablution round earth's human shores,
Or gazing on the new soft-fallen mask
   Of snow upon the mountains and the moors—
No—yet still steadfast, still unchangeable,
   Pillowed upon my fair love's ripening breast,
To feel for ever its soft fall and swell,
   Awake for ever in a sweet unrest,
     Still, still to hear her tender-taken breath,
     And so live ever—or else swoon to death.

with eternal lids apart] i.e. with uninterrupted watching
Eremite] religious recluse, hermit
ablution] washing

7

Love (III)

GEORGE HERBERT

Love bade me welcome: yet my soul drew back,
        Guilty of dust and sin.
But quick-eyed Love, observing me grow slack
        From my first entrance in,
Drew nearer to me, sweetly questioning,
        If I lacked anything.

A guest, I answered, worthy to be here:
        Love said, You shall be he.
I the unkind, ungrateful? Ah my dear,
        I cannot look on thee.
Love took my hand, and smiling did reply,
        Who made the eyes but I?

Truth Lord, but I have marred them: let my shame
        Go where it doth deserve.
And know you not, says Love, who bore the blame?
        My dear, then I will serve.
You must sit down, says Love, and taste my meat:
        So I did sit and eat.

FINIS.

*Glory be to God on high, and on earth
peace, good will towards men.*

grow slack] become remiss, negligent

8

Lovers' Infiniteness

JOHN DONNE

If yet I have not all thy love,
Dear, I shall never have it all,
I cannot breathe one other sigh, to move,
Nor can entreat one other tear to fall.
All my treasure, which should purchase thee,
Sighs, tears, and oaths, and letters I have spent,
Yet no more can be due to me,
Than at the bargain made was meant.
If then thy gift of love were partial,
That some to me, some should to others fall,
   Dear, I shall never have thee all.

Or if then thou gavest me all,
All was but all, which thou hadst then;
But if in thy heart, since, there be or shall
New love created be, by other men,
Which have their stocks entire, and can in tears,
In sighs, in oaths, and letters outbid me,
This new love may beget new fears,
For, this love was not vowed by thee.
And yet it was, thy gift being general,
The ground, thy heart is mine; whatever shall
   Grow there, dear, I should have it all.

stocks entire] undiminished store
general] indifferently offered

Yet I would not have all yet,
He that hath all can have no more,
And since my love doth every day admit
New growth, thou shouldst have new rewards in store;
Thou canst not every day give me thy heart,
If thou canst give it, then thou never gav'st it:
Love's riddles are, that though thy heart depart,
It stays at home, and thou with losing sav'st it:
But we will have a way more liberal,
Than changing hearts, to join them, so we shall
   Be one, and one another's all.

Love's riddles . . . losing sav'st it] it is the paradox of love that in giving your heart to another, it
  is transfigured; and compare Matthew 16, 25, where Jesus says: 'For whosoever will save his
  life shall lose it: and whosoever will lose his life for my sake shall find it'

9

The Bargain

SIR PHILIP SIDNEY

My true love hath my heart, and I have his,
    By just exchange, one for the other given.
I hold his dear, and mine he cannot miss,
    There never was a better bargain driven.
His heart in me keeps me and him in one,
    My heart in him his thoughts and senses guides;
He loves my heart, for once it was his own,
    I cherish his, because in me it bides.
His heart his wound receivèd from my sight,
    My heart was wounded with his wounded heart;
For as from me on him his hurt did light,
    So still methought in me his hurt did smart.
        Both equal hurt, in this change sought our bliss:
        My true love hath my heart and I have his.

cannot miss] can scarcely fail to acknowledge
bides] stays, abides
his wound] i.e. his heart's wound
hurt did light] received his wound
change] exchange

10

To My Dear and Loving Husband

ANNE BRADSTREET

If ever two were one, then surely we.
If ever man were lov'd by wife, then thee;
If ever wife was happy in a man,
Compare with me ye women if you can.
I prize thy love more than whole Mines of gold,
Or all the riches that the East doth hold.
My love is such that Rivers cannot quench,
Nor aught but love from thee, give recompense.
Thy love is such I can no way repay,
The heavens reward thee manifold I pray.
Then while we live, in love lets so perséver,
That when we live no more, we may live ever.

11

'She was a Phantom of Delight'

WILLIAM WORDSWORTH

She was a Phantom of delight
When first she gleamed upon my sight;
A lovely Apparition, sent
To be a moment's ornament;
Her eyes as stars of Twilight fair;
Like Twilight's, too, her dusky hair;
But all things else about her drawn
From May-time and the chearful Dawn;
A dancing Shape, an Image gay,
To haunt, to startle, and way-lay.

I saw her upon nearer view,
A Spirit, yet a Woman too!
Her household motions light and free,
And steps of virgin liberty;
A countenance in which did meet
Sweet records, promises as sweet;
A Creature not too bright or good
For human nature's daily food;
For transient sorrows, simple wiles,
Praise, blame, love, kisses, tears, and smiles.

And now I see with eye serene
The very pulse of the machine;
A Being breathing thoughtful breath;
A Traveller betwixt life and death;
The reason firm, the temperate will,
Endurance, foresight, strength and skill;
A perfect Woman; nobly planned,
To warn, to comfort, and command;
And yet a Spirit still, and bright
With something of an angel light.

household motions] domestic activity   temperate will] moderate ambition

12

If Thou must Love Me

ELIZABETH BARRETT BROWNING

If thou must love me, let it be for nought
Except for love's sake only. Do not say
"I love her for her smile .. her look .. her way
Of speaking gently ..; for a trick of thought
That falls in well with mine, and certes brought
A sense of pleasant ease on such a day—"
For these things in themselves, beloved, may
Be changed, or change for thee, .. and love so wrought,
May be unwrought so. Neither love me for
Thine own dear pity wiping my cheeks dry!—
For one might well forget to weep, who bore
Thy comfort long, and lose thy love thereby—
But love me for love's sake, that evermore
Thou may'st love on through love's eternity—

certes] certainly, assuredly
bore | Thy comfort long] has been receiving your tender reassurances for so long

13

The Wedding

MONIZA ALVI

I expected a quiet wedding
high above a lost city
a marriage to balance on my head

like a forest of sticks, a pot of water.
The ceremony tasted of nothing
had little colour – guests arrived

  stealthy as sandalwood smugglers.
When they opened their suitcases
England spilled out.

They scratched at my veil
like beggars on a car window.
I insisted my dowry was simple –

a smile, a shadow, a whisper,
my house an incredible structure
of stiffened rags and bamboo.

We travelled along roads with English
names, my bridegroom and I.
Our eyes changed colour

like traffic-lights, so they said.
The time was not ripe
for us to view each other.

We stared straight ahead as if
we could see through mountains
breathe life into new cities.

I wanted to marry a country
take up a river for a veil
sing in the Jinnah Gardens

hold up my dream, tricky
as a snake-charmer's snake.
Our thoughts half-submerged

like buffaloes under dark water
we turned and faced each other
with turbulence

and imprints like maps on our hands.

Jinnah Gardens] a pleasure park in Lahore, Pakistan

14

Tiger in the Menagerie

EMMA JONES

No one could say how the tiger got into the menagerie.
It was too flash, too blue,
too much like the painting of a tiger.

At night the bars of the cage and the stripes of the tiger
looked into each other so long
that when it was time for those eyes to rock shut

the bars were the lashes of the stripes
the stripes were the lashes of the bars

and they walked together in their dreams so long
through the long colonnade
that shed its fretwork to the Indian main

that when the sun rose they'd gone and the tiger was
one clear orange eye that walked into the menagerie.

No one could say how the tiger got out in the menagerie.
It was too bright, too bare.
If the menagerie could, it would say 'tiger'.

If the aviary could, it would lock its door.
Its heart began to beat in rows of rising birds
when the tiger came inside to wait.

main] ocean

15

The Pride of Lions

JOANNA PRESTON

But before we could marry, he became a lion –
thick pelted, and rich with the musk of beast.

The switch to all fours was not easy – all his weight
slung from the blades of his shoulders.
His deltoids knotted like teak burls,
and I burnished them as he slept.

Burrs matted his mane, and for days
he wouldn't let me groom him –
slapped me away with a suede paw,
snarled against my throat.

He would not eat fruit, or drink milk,
but tore meat from the bones I provided.

His claws caught in the carpet,
so I stripped the rugs from the floor
and polished the boards until they gleamed
and rang with the chime of his nails.

I stroke his saffron hide
and tangle my fingers deep in his ruff,
draw him up around me, ardent
as the gleam of his topaz eyes

– the hypnotic lash of his tail,
the rasp of his tongue on my thighs.

16

lion heart

AMANDA CHONG

You came out of the sea,
skin dappled scales of sunlight;
Riding crests, waves of fish in your fists.
Washed up, your gills snapped shut.
Water whipped the first breath of your lungs,
Your lips' bud teased by morning mists.

You conquered the shore, its ivory coast.
Your legs still rocked with the memory of waves.
Sinews of sand ran across your back–
Rising runes of your oceanic origins.
Your heart thumped– an animal skin drum
heralding the coming of a prince.

In the jungle, amid rasping branches,
trees loosened their shadows to shroud you.
The prince beheld you then, a golden sheen.
Your eyes, two flickers; emerald blaze
You settled back on fluent haunches;
The squall of a beast, your roar, your call.

In crackling boats, seeds arrived, wind-blown,
You summoned their colours to the palm
of your hand, folded them snugly into loam,
watched saplings swaddled in green,
as they sunk roots, spawned shade,
and embraced the land that embraced them.

runes] enigmatic lettering

Centuries, by the sea's pulmonary,
a vein throbbing humming bumboats–
your trees rise as skyscrapers.
Their ankles lost in swilling water,
as they heave themselves higher
above the mirrored surface.

Remember your self: your raw lion heart,
Each beat a stony echo that washes
through ribbed vaults of buildings.

Remember your keris, iron lightning
ripping through tentacles of waves,
double-edged, curved to a point–

flung high and caught unsheathed, scattering
five stars in the red tapestry of your sky.

keris] swords with a curved, wave-like blade   bumboats] small boats, junks

17

To Mrs. Reynolds's Cat

JOHN KEATS

Cat! who hast past thy Grand Climacteric,
 How many mice and Rats hast in thy days
 Destroy'd?—how many tit bits stolen? Gaze
With those bright languid segments green and prick
Those velvet ears—but pr'ythee do not stick
 Thy latent talons in me—and upraise
 Thy gentle mew—and tell me all thy frays
Of Fish and Mice, and Rats and tender chick.
Nay look not down, nor lick thy dainty wrists—
 For all the weezy Asthma,—and for all
Thy tail's tip is nicked off—and though the fists
 Of many a Maid have given thee many a maul,
Still is that fur as soft as when the lists
 In youth thou enter'dst on glass-bottled wall.

Grand Climacteric] the supposedly critical age in the seven-year stages of human life (63 being its
    ninth, cats supposedly having nine lives)
maul] beating
the lists . . . thou enter'dst] you entered the lists (i.e. took part in tournaments or jousts)
glass-bottled wall] i.e. a wall defended from intruders by fragments of broken glass

18

Sonnet 19

WILLIAM SHAKESPEARE

Devouring Time, blunt thou the lion's paws,
And make the earth devour her own sweet brood;
Pluck the keen teeth from the fierce tiger's jaws,
And burn the long-liv'd Phoenix in her blood;
Make glad and sorry seasons as thou fleets,
And do whate'er thou wilt, swift-footed Time,
To the wide world and all her fading sweets;
But I forbid thee one more heinous crime:
O, carve not with the hours my love's fair brow,
Nor draw no lines there with thine antique pen!
Him in thy course untainted do allow
For beauty's pattern to succeeding men.
  Yet do thy worst, old Time! Despite thy wrong
  My love shall in my verse ever live young.

the long-liv'd Phoenix] a single mythical bird believed to live for 500 years, then burn itself on a
   pyre, before being born again from its ashes
antique] (1) old; (2) deranged
beauty's pattern to succeeding men] the model of beauty for succeeding generations
thy wrong] your damage

19

Heart and Mind

EDITH SITWELL

Said the Lion to the Lioness—'When you are amber dust,—
No more a raging fire like the heat of the Sun
(No liking but all lust)—
Remember still the flowering of the amber blood and bone,
The rippling of bright muscles like a sea,
Remember the rose-prickles of bright paws
Though we shall mate no more
Till the fire of that sun the heart and the moon-cold bone are one.'

Said the Skeleton lying upon the sands of Time—
'The great gold planet that is the mourning heat of the Sun
Is greater than all gold, more powerful
Than the tawny body of a Lion that fire consumes
Like all that grows or leaps . . . so is the heart

More powerful than all dust. Once I was Hercules
Or Samson, strong as the pillars of the seas:
But the flames of the heart consumed me, and the mind
Is but a foolish wind.'

Said the Sun to the Moon—'When you are but a lonely white crone,
And I, a dead King in my golden armour somewhere in a dark wood,
Remember only this of our hopeless love
That never till Time is done
Will the fire of the heart and the fire of the mind be one.'

Hercules . . . Samson] the strongman superheroes of Greek mythology and the Bible, each of
    whom was betrayed and undone by love
the pillars of the seas] the supposed boundary-columns at the entrance to the Mediterranean

20

For My Grandmother Knitting

LIZ LOCHHEAD

There is no need they say
but the needles still move
their rhythms in the working of your hands
as easily
as if your hands
were once again those sure and skilful hands
of the fisher-girl.

You are old now
and your grasp of things is not so good
but master of your moments then
deft and swift
you slit the still-ticking quick silver fish.
Hard work it was too
of necessity.

But now they say there is no need
as the needles move
in the working of your hands
once the hands of the bride
with the hand-span waist
once the hands of the miner's wife
who scrubbed his back
in a tin bath by the coal fire
once the hands of the mother
of six who made do and mended
scraped and slaved slapped sometimes
when necessary.

still-ticking] i.e. still alive
hand-span] i.e. impossibly slim

But now they say there is no need
the kids they say grandma
have too much already
more than they can wear
too many scarves and cardigans –
gran you do too much
there's no necessity.

21

The Uncles

JOHN GOODBY

[handwritten: → a Professor / → higher class]

[handwritten: Car, Mechanics]

[handwritten: → technical terms, their know-how]

Uncles, talking the camshaft or the gimbal connected
to a slowly oscillating crank. The Uncles Brickell,
Swarfega kings, enseamed with swarf and scobs, skin
measled with gunmetal but glistening faintly, loud
in the smoke. Lithe and wiry above the lathe, milling out
a cylinder to a given bore. Uncles, pencil-stubs at their ears,
spurning ink, crossing sevens like émigré intellectuals,
measuring in thous and thirty-secondths (scrawled
on torn fag-packets); feinting with slide rules, racing,
but mild not as mild steel. Pockets congested, always. Uncles
with dockets for jobs, corners transparent with grease,
with a light machine oil. Time-served, my Uncles, branch-
ing out into doorhandles, grub-screws and the brass bits
that hold the front of the motor case to the rear flange
of the mounting panel. Release tab. Slightly hard of hearing
now, the Uncles, from the din of the shop, slowly nodding.

[handwritten: mess]
[handwritten: respect]
[handwritten: elevating handiman / degrees, technicality + precision]
[handwritten: Personal]
[handwritten: Sport found, release, contented]
[handwritten: Free verse → messiness, yet punctuation]

camshaft . . . gimbal] driving rod . . . connecting joint
Swarfega] a viscous hand-detergent
swarf and scobs] oily dirt and shavings
bore] diameter
crossing sevens] i.e. writing the numeral '7' with a horizontal stroke (in the European way)
thous] thousandths (of an inch)
mild . . . mild steel] gentle . . . a particularly strong alloy of steel
grub-screw] a technical kind of screw
flange . . . mounting panel] i.e. components of an engine
Release tab] perhaps the opening of the 'tab' on a can of beer

ordered clutter

List

← sense

non-aesthetic urban

order/chaos duality

undetailed

Don't fear technology

wholesome, changing times

as figures

proud

Uncles in 'Red Square'; uncles swapping tolerance gauges,
allan keys, telephone numbers, deals and rank commun-
ism. Forefingers describing arcs and cutting angles. White
and milky with coolants and lubricants, mess of order. Never
forgetting to ply a broom after. The missing half-finger, not
really missed any longer, just a banjo-hand gone west. My
Uncles still making a go of mower blades, on the road
at their age; offering cigars at Christmas. Uncanny if
encountered in visors, overalls, confounding nephews
in dignity of their calling, their epoch-stewed tea. Stand
a spoon in all their chamfered years, cut short or long. Uncles
immortal in the welding shed, under neon, lounge
as the vast doors slide to a cool blue dusk. My Uncles.

'Red Square'] the central square in Moscow (until 1991 the capital of the Soviet Union)
tolerance gauges, allan keys] i.e. various engineering tools
ply a broom] i.e. do the sweeping up
gone west] (*slang*) i.e. 'gone for a burton', 'bought it' (i.e. of wartime airmen who were lost in
    action or 'went missing')
epoch-stewed] i.e. left to stew for ages
chamfered] bevelled, planed

22

Surplus Value

DAVID C. WARD

My Michigan brother-in-law was a tool and die guy,
A machinist, fabricating parts in shops supplying Big Three
Auto makers. A bantam with thick fingers, scarred hands
He rode a Harley soft-tail, drank Iron City, and lived
With his wife and kids in a house he mostly built himself.
During the heyday of Detroit metal, overtime and union
Contracts paid for steaks and a cabin on an upstate lake
For summer vacations and deer season hunting trips
In the fall. He took his pride from his craft and skill
Building something bigger than the Fords or Chevys
He pushed on down the line for America to drive.
For twenty years of work, good times, and happy with it.
But that road ran out. The union went south first
(pension fraud; indictments; prison terms) and then
The companies and their money men slashed and burned
Their way through labor and its costs in search of market
Share. The work was sweated from the men for less and less return.
From economy of scale, to one of scarcity: subcontracting, piecework,
Ultimately the dole replaced a steady pay check and a bonus
Twice a year. The Harley went and then the cabin; food stamps
Bought essentials, nothing more. Always quiet, he grew quieter
From day to week to month to the years that stretched ahead,
Bowing his neck each day as the scars grew deeper now, and inward.

During the boom that no one thought would ever end,
Heedless the factories flushed their waste straight into
The Saginaw River, so much so that it never iced, even
In the depths of winter. Now it's frozen all year long.

bantam] literally a small but muscular variety of chicken; hence slender but strong
Harley soft-tail] a make of motorcycle
Iron City] a brand of beer
Fords or Chevys] makes of car
went south] collapsed, lost power, 'went belly-up'
food stamps] welfare payments
Saginaw River] in Michigan

23

Father Returning Home

DILIP CHITRE

My father travels on the late evening train
Standing among silent commuters in the yellow light
Suburbs slide past his unseeing eyes
His shirt and pants are soggy and his black raincoat
Stained with mud and his bag stuffed with books
Is falling apart. His eyes dimmed by age
fade homeward through the humid monsoon night.
Now I can see him getting off the train
Like a word dropped from a long sentence.
He hurries across the length of the grey platform,
Crosses the railway line, enters the lane,
His chappals are sticky with mud, but he hurries onward.
Home again, I see him drinking weak tea,
Eating a stale chapati, reading a book.
He goes into the toilet to contemplate
Man's estrangement from a man-made world.
Coming out he trembles at the sink,
The cold water running over his brown hands,
A few droplets cling to the greying hairs on his wrists.
His sullen children have often refused to share
Jokes and secrets with him. He will now go to sleep
Listening to the static on the radio, dreaming
Of his ancestors and grandchildren, thinking
Of nomads entering a subcontinent through a narrow pass.

chappals] leather sandals
chapati] piece of unleavened bread

24

In the Park

GWEN HARWOOD

She sits in the park. Her clothes are out of date.
Two children whine and bicker, tug her skirt.
A third draws aimless patterns in the dirt.
Someone she loved once passes by – too late

to feign indifference to that casual nod.
"How nice," et cetera. "Time holds great surprises."
From his neat head unquestionably rises
a small balloon… "but for the grace of God…"

They stand a while in flickering light, rehearsing
the children's names and birthdays. "It's so sweet
to hear their chatter, watch them grow and thrive,"
she says to his departing smile. Then, nursing
the youngest child, sits staring at her feet.
To the wind she says, "They have eaten me alive."

a small balloon] i.e. the convention in comics and graphic novels to signal thoughts by supplying
their words in a cloud-like balloon above the character thinking them

25

The Lost Woman...

PATRICIA BEER

My mother went with no more warning
than a bright voice and a bad pain
Home from school on a June morning
And where the brook goes under the lane
I saw the back of a shocking white
Ambulance drawing away from the gate.

She never returned and I never saw
Her buried. So a romance began.
The ivy-mother turned into a tree
That still hops away like a rainbow down
The avenue as I approach.
My tendrils are the ones that clutch.

I made a life for her over the years.
Frustrated no more by a dull marriage
She ran a canteen through several wars.
The wit of a cliché-ridden village
She met her match at an extra-mural
Class and the OU summer school.

Many a hero in his time
And every poet has acquired
A lost woman to haunt the home,
To be compensated and desired,
Who will not alter, who will not grow
A corpse they need never get to know.

OU] the Open University (the British distance-learning university)

She is nearly always benign. Her habit
Is not to stride at dead of night.
Soft and crepuscular in rabbit-
Light she comes out. Hear how they hate
Themselves for losing her as they did.
Her country is bland and she does not chide.

But my lost woman evermore snaps
From somewhere else: 'you did not love me.
I sacrificed too much perhaps,
I showed you the way to rise above me
And you took it. You are the ghost
With the bat-voice, my dear. I am not lost.'

26

Stabat Mater

SAM HUNT

My mother called my father 'Mr Hunt'
For the first few years of married life.
I learned this from a book she had inscribed:
'To dear Mr Hunt, from his loving wife.'

She was embarrassed when I asked her why
But later on explained how hard it had been
To call him any other name at first, when he –
Her father's elder – made her seem so small.

Now in a different way, still like a girl,
She calls my father every other sort of name;
And guiding him as he roams old age
Sometimes turns to me as if it were a game . . .

That once I stand up straight, I too must learn
To walk away and know there's no return.

Stabat Mater] (Latin: 'The mother stood'); the title of a medieval hymn to Mary, the grieving
    mother of Jesus

27

Coming Home

OWEN SHEERS

My mother's hug is awkward,
as if the space between her open arms
is reserved for a child, not this body of a man.
In the kitchen she kneads the dough,
flipping it and patting before laying in again.
The flour makes her over, dusting
the hairs on her cheek, smoothing out wrinkles.

*

Dad still goes and soaks himself in the rain.
Up to his elbows in hedge, he works
on a hole that reappears every Winter,
its edges laced with wet wool –
frozen breaths snagged on the blackthorn.
When he comes in again his hair is wild,
and his pockets are filled with filings of hay.

*

All seated, my grandfather pours the wine.
His unsteady hand makes the neck of the bottle
shiver on the lip of each glass;
it is a tune he plays faster each year.

makes her over] transforms her appearance, gives her a glamorous 'makeover'

28

On My First Daughter

(handwritten: Epitaph)   BEN JONSON *(handwritten: → Shakespeare's contemporary / → Time of infant mortality?)*

(handwritten left margin: Can go to heaven / ↑ → Anglicans baptise / Baptism earlier than / Catholics / ↓ / sincere Belief in heaven / Sincerity / Maternity / Mary's child (Jesus) died)

(handwritten: Grave)
Here lies, to each her parents' ruth,
Mary, the daughter of their youth; *(handwritten: young couple, their own innocence)*
Yet all heaven's gifts being heaven's due, *(handwritten: Fated?   God loans life. Must return.)*
It makes the father less to rue. *(handwritten: euphemistic   God's Plan)*
At six months' end she parted hence
With safety of her innocence;
Whose soul heaven's queen, whose name she bears, *(handwritten: Pure)*
In comfort of her mother's tears,
Hath placed amongst her virgin-train:
Where, while that severed doth remain, *(handwritten: Parents)*
This grave partakes the fleshly birth; *(handwritten: raw, pain of childbirth echoes)*
Which cover lightly, gentle earth! *(handwritten: Burial)*

(handwritten: Rhyme Couplets, Parents / nursery-ish)

(handwritten: Closure, acceptance)

(handwritten: Tender Explanation of God's Plan)

each her] i.e. both her
ruth] sorrow
heaven's gifts being heaven's due] i.e. all life being on loan from God, and therefore
    owed back
makes the father less to rue] assuages a father's sorrow
safety of her innocence] i.e. destined for heaven by reason of her innocence
heaven's queen] i.e. Mary, mother of Jesus
virgin-train] retinue of maidens
Which cover lightly] i.e. which (I beg you to) gently cover over

29

Sons, Departing

JOHN CASSIDY

They walked away between tall hedges,
their heads just clear and blond
with sunlight, the hedges' dark sides
sickly with drifts of flowers.

They were facing the sea and miles
of empty air; the sky had high
torn clouds, the sea its irregular
runs and spatters of white.

They did not look back; the steadiness
of their retreating footfalls lapsed
in a long diminuendo; their line
was straight as the clipped privets.

They looked at four sliding gulls
a long way up, scattering down frail
complaints; the fickle wind filled in
with sounds of town and distance.

They became sunlit points; in a broad
Haphazard world the certain focus.
Against the random patterns of the sea
their walk was one-dimensional, and final.

diminuendo] a musical term instructing a decreasing in volume

Part 2

Birds, Beasts, and the Weather

30

In Praise of Creation

ELIZABETH JENNINGS

That one bird, one star,
The one flash of the tiger's eye
Purely assert what they are,
Without ceremony testify.

Testify to order, to rule–
How the birds mate at one time only,
How the sky is, for a certain time, full
Of birds, the moon sometimes cut thinly.

And the tiger trapped in the cage of his skin,
Watchful over creation, rests
For the blood to pound, the drums to begin,
Till the tigress' shadow casts

A darkness over him, a passion, a scent,
The world goes turning, turning, the season
Sieves earth to its one sure element
And the blood beats beyond reason.

Then quiet, and birds folding their wings,
The new moon waiting for years to be stared at here,
The season sinks to satisfied things–
Man with his mind ajar.

31

Upon a Wasp Chilled with Cold

EDWARD TAYLOR

The Bear that breathes the Northern blast
Did numb, Torpedo like, a Wasp
Whose stiffend limbs encrampt, lay bathing
In Sol's warm breath and shine as saving,
Which with her hands she chafes and stands
Rubbing her Legs, Shanks, Thighs, and hands.
Her petty toes, and fingers ends
Nipt with this breath, she out extends
Unto the Sun, in greate desire
To warm her digits at that fire.
Doth hold her Temples in this state
Where pulse doth beate, and head doth ake.
Doth turn, and stretch her body small,
Doth Comb her velvet Capitall.
As if her little brain pan were
A Volume of Choice precepts cleare.
As if her sattin jacket hot
Contained Apothecaries Shop
Of Natures recepts, that prevails
To remedy all her sad ailes,
As if her velvet helmet high
Did turret rationality.

The Bear] the constellation Ursa Major, associated with the North Star, hence with cold winds
Torpedo like] i.e. struck by the numbing electrical charge emitted by a species of ray
Sol's] the sun's
Capitall] head
brain pan] skull
Volume of Choice precepts cleare] book of exemplary moral instruction
Apothecaries Shop . . . Natures recepts] pharmacy . . . natural herbal remedies
turret rationality] form a fortress of reason

She fans her wing up to the Winde
As if her Pettycoate were lin'de,
With reasons fleece, and hoises sails
And hu'ming flies in thankfull gails
Unto her dun Curld palace Hall
Her warm thanks offering for all.

Lord cleare my misted sight that I
May hence view thy Divinity.
Some sparkes whereof thou up dost hasp
Within this little downy Wasp
In whose small Corporation wee
A school and a schoolmaster see
Where we may learn, and easily finde
A nimble Spirit bravely minde
Her worke in ev'ry limb: and lace
It up neate with a vitall grace,
Acting each part though ne'er so small
Here of this Fustian animall.
Till I enravisht Climb into
The Godhead on this Ladder doe.
Where all my pipes inspir'de upraise
An Heavenly musick furrd with praise.

Pettycoate] chemise, undergarment
hoises sails] hoists up her sails
hasp] secure, instil
small Corporation] miniature organisation of bodily components
Fustian] precocious (because overdressed)
Till I enravisht Climb . . . doe] Until I myself climb and enter a state of divine bliss
pipes] musical instruments

32

Taking Back

JACK UNDERWOOD

Wasn't it great to feed old Tabitha,
the eating plant? Stunning the bugs
with a fizzing blue light, fobbing them down
the fun-pipe of our hungry hungry-queen.

Next day there was never any sign,
no wing-clot or stray leg in sight,
not even scorch marks on the bulb;
old Tabitha had licked the whole room clean.

We had to move out, so chucked her in a skip.
What's left of those nights lifts a leaf or leg
beneath the fudge of old bins.

I imagine finding her again, jaws open,
aghast. But that's the trouble with the past;
you can never take back the things you put in.

33

'Blessed by the Indifference...' from The Flowers of Crete

CHRISTOPHER REID

Blessed by the indifference of the creatures –
big, sting-toting insects on haphazard reconnaissance,
scampering ants with their matching shadows
        scampering under them,
the squeaky-wheel bird in some tree, and the one
with the white throat and flight
        full of flusters and feints –
we take our breakfast of coffee and yoghurt out in the sun.

Even the sun, that more dangerous beast, has begun
his morning prowl in a spirit of negligent generosity,
not seeming to mind, or to want to murder us, much,
but laying the landscape out in its ancient
        shapes and colours,
velvety ochres and greens on the steep hill,
        a blue-green
glaze on the bay, as if to say,
'These are my wares. Yours more or less for the asking.
Of course I accept your paltry currency, your small change
        of days and hours.'

34

Australia 1970

JUDITH WRIGHT

Die, wild country, like the eaglehawk,
dangerous till the last breath's gone,
clawing and striking. Die
cursing your captor through a raging eye.

Die like the tigersnake
that hisses such pure hatred from its pain
as fills the killer's dreams
with fear like suicide's invading stain.

Suffer, wild country, like the ironwood
that gaps the dozer-blade.
I see your living soil ebb with the tree
to naked poverty.

Die like the soldier-ant
mindless and faithful to your million years.
Though we corrupt you with our torturing mind,
stay obstinate; stay blind.

For we are conquerors and self-poisoners
more than scorpion or snake
and dying of the venoms that we make
even while you die of us.

I praise the scoring drought, the flying dust,
the drying creek, the furious animal,
that they oppose us still;
that we are ruined by the thing we kill.

ironwood] hardwood tree
gaps the dozer-blade] i.e. even chips the shovels of bulldozers

35

The Poplar-Field

WILLIAM COWPER

The poplars are felled, farewell to the shade
And the whispering sound of the cool colonnade,
The winds play no longer, and sing in the leaves,
Nor Ouse on his bosom their image receives.

Twelve years have elapsed since I last took a view
Of my favourite field and the bank where they grew,
And now in the grass behold they are laid,
And the tree is my seat that once lent me a shade.

The blackbird has fled to another retreat
Where the hazels afford him a screen from the heat,
And the scene where his melody charmed me before,
Resounds with his sweet-flowing ditty no more.

My fugitive years are all hasting away,
And I must ere long lie as lowly as they,
With a turf on my breast, and a stone at my head,
Ere another such grove shall arise in its stead.

'Tis a sight to engage me, if any thing can,
To muse on the perishing pleasures of man;
Though his life be a dream, his enjoyments, I see,
Have a being less durable even than he.

Ouse on his bosom] i.e. the surface (or heart) of the East Anglian River Ouse
the tree is my seat] i.e. the wood from the felled tree was made into the chair I now sit in

36

Ode on Melancholy

JOHN KEATS

I

No, no, go not to Lethe, neither twist
   Wolf's-bane, tight-rooted, for its poisonous wine;
Nor suffer thy pale forehead to be kiss'd
   By nightshade, ruby grape of Proserpine;
Make not your rosary of yew-berries,
    Nor let the beetle, nor the death-moth be
      Your mournful Psyche, nor the downy owl
A partner in your sorrow's mysteries;
    For shade to shade will come too drowsily,
      And drown the wakeful anguish of the soul.

II

But when the melancholy fit shall fall
   Sudden from heaven like a weeping cloud,
That fosters the droop-headed flowers all,
   And hides the green hill in an April shroud;
Then glut thy sorrow on a morning rose,
    Or on the rainbow of the salt sand-wave,
      Or on the wealth of globed peonies;
Or if thy mistress some rich anger shows,
    Emprison her soft hand, and let her rave,
      And feed deep, deep upon her peerless eyes.

Lethe] in classical mythology, the river of forgetfulness
Wolf's-bane . . . nightshade] poisonous plants
Proserpine] in classical mythology, the goddess of the underworld
yew-berries] berries of the yew tree, also poisonous, and often planted in churchyards
beetle . . . death-moth . . . owl] i.e. emblems of the dark night of life
Psyche] the winged embodiment of the soul

III

She dwells with Beauty—Beauty that must die;
   And Joy, whose hand is ever at his lips
Bidding adieu; and aching Pleasure nigh,
   Turning to poison while the bee-mouth sips:
Ay, in the very temple of Delight
    Veil'd Melancholy has her sovran shrine,
     Though seen of none save him whose strenuous tongue
Can burst Joy's grape against his palate fine;
   His soul shall taste the sadness of her might,
    And be among her cloudy trophies hung.

37

Description of Spring

HENRY HOWARD, EARL OF SURREY

The soote season, that bud and bloom forth brings,
With green hath clad the hill, and eke the vale.
The nightingale with feathers new she sings;
The turtle to her make hath told her tale.
Summer is come, for every spray now springs,
The hart hath hung his old head on the pale;
The buck in brake his winter coat he slings;
The fishes flete with new repairèd scale;
The adder all her slough away she slings;
The swift swallow pursueth the fliës smale;
The busy bee her honey now she mings;
Winter is worn that was the flowers' bale.
    And thus I see among these pleasant things
    Each care decays, and yet my sorrow springs!

soote] sweet
eke the vale] also the valley
turtle] turtle-dove
make] companion, mate
hart] mature male deer
pale] enclosing fence
buck] young male deer
brake] thicket of woodland
flete] float, swim
fliës smale] i.e. small flies (but pronounced as two syllables: 'fly-es')
mings] blends, mixes, brews
bale] destruction

38

The Spring

THOMAS CAREW

Now that the winter's gone, the earth hath lost
Her snow-white robes; and now no more the frost
Candies the grass, or casts an icy cream
Upon the silver lake or crystal stream:
But the warm sun thaws the benumbed earth,
And makes it tender; gives a sacred birth
To the dead swallow; wakes in hollow tree
The drowsy cuckoo and the humble-bee.
Now do a choir of chirping minstrels bring,
In triumph to the world, the youthful spring:
The valleys, hills, and woods in rich array
Welcome the coming of the long'd-for May.
Now all things smile: only my love doth lower,
Nor hath the scalding noon-day sun the power
To melt that marble ice, which still doth hold
Her heart congeal'd, and makes her pity cold.
The ox, which lately did for shelter fly
Into the stall, doth now securely lie
In open fields; and love no more is made
By the fire-side, but in the cooler shade.
Amyntas now doth with his Chloris sleep
Under a sycamore, and all things keep
Time with the season: only she doth carry
June in her eyes, in her heart January.

Candies] sugars over (as if with icing sugar)
gives a sacred birth | To the dead swallow] i.e. resurrects the year with the first birdsong of spring
lower] (pronounced to rhyme with 'power') sulk, pout
Amyntas . . . Chloris] the generic classical names for rustic lovers
June . . . January] i.e. with a warm welcome, but a cold prospect

39

Coming

PHILIP LARKIN

On longer evenings,
Light, chill and yellow,
Bathes the serene
Foreheads of houses.
A thrush sings,
Laurel-surrounded
In the deep bare garden,
Its fresh-peeled voice
Astonishing the brickwork.
It will be spring soon,
It will be spring soon—
And I, whose childhood
Is a forgotten boredom,
Feel like a child
Who comes on a scene
Of adult reconciling,
And can understand nothing
But the unusual laughter,
And starts to be happy.

40

The Darkling Thrush

THOMAS HARDY

I leant upon a coppice gate
When Frost was spectre-grey,
And Winter's dregs made desolate
   The weakening eye of day.
The tangled bine-stems scored the sky
   Like strings of broken lyres,
And all mankind that haunted nigh
   Had sought their household fires.
The land's sharp features seemed to be
   The Century's corpse outleant,
His crypt the cloudy canopy,
   The wind his death-lament.
The ancient pulse of germ and birth
   Was shrunken hard and dry,
And every spirit upon earth
   Seemed fervourless as I.
At once a voice arose among
   The bleak twigs overhead
In a full-hearted evensong
   Of joy illimited;
An aged thrush, frail, gaunt and small,
   In blast-beruffled plume,
Had chosen thus to fling his soul
   Upon the growing gloom.

Darkling] in the dark
coppice] a cultivated thicket of trees
bine-stems] tendrils, climbing shoots
lyres] harp-like stringed instruments
crypt . . . canopy] tomb . . . enclosing sky
germ] seed
evensong] literally a song of twilight; the Christian church service (also known as vespers)

So little cause for carolings
    Of such ecstatic sound
Was written on terrestrial things
    Afar or nigh around,
That I could think there trembled through
    His happy good-night air
Some blessed Hope, whereof he knew
    And I was unaware.

41

Stormcock in Elder

RUTH PITTER

In my dark hermitage, aloof
From the world's sight and the world's sound,
By the small door where the old roof
Hangs but five feet above the ground,
I groped along the shelf for bread
But found celestial food instead:

For suddenly close at my ear,
Loud, loud and wild, with wintry glee,
The old unfailing chorister
Burst out in pride of poetry;
And through the broken roof I spied
Him by his singing glorified.

Scarcely an arm's-length from the eye,
Myself unseen, I saw him there;
The throbbing throat that made the cry,
The breast dewed from the misty air,
The polished bill that opened wide
And showed the pointed tongue inside;

The large eye, ringed with many a ray
Of minion feathers, finely laid,
The feet that grasped the elder-spray;
How strongly used, how subtly made
The scale, the sinew, and the claw,
Plain through the broken roof I saw;

Stormcock] a singing bird, also known as the missel-thrush
hermitage] secluded house
minion] elegant

The flight-feathers in tail and wing,
The shorter coverts, and the white
Merged into russet, marrying
The bright breast to the pinions bright,
Gold sequins, spots of chestnut, shower
Of silver, like a brindled flower.

Soldier of fortune, northwest Jack,
Old hard-times' braggart, there you blow
But tell me ere your bagpipes crack
How you can make so brave a show,
Full-fed in February, and dressed
Like a rich merchant at a feast.

One-half the world, or so they say,
Knows not how half the world may live;
So sing your song and go your way,
And still in February contrive
As bright as Gabriel to smile
On elder-spray by broken tile.

coverts] short feathers (at the base of larger ones)
pinions] wing feathers
Gabriel] the angel Gabriel (often depicted with a horn or trumpet summoning repentance)

42

The Caged Skylark

GERARD MANLEY HOPKINS

As a dare-gale skylark scanted in a dull cage,
　　Man's mounting spirit in his bone-house, mean house, dwells –
　　That bird beyond the remembering his free fells;
This in drudgery, day-labouring-out life's age.
Though aloft on turf or perch or poor low stage
　　Both sing sometímes the sweetest, sweetest spells,
　　Yet both droop deadly sómetimes in their cells
Or wring their barriers in bursts of fear or rage.

Not that the sweet-fowl, song-fowl, needs no rest –
Why, hear him, hear him babble and drop down to his nest,
　　But his own nest, wild nest, no prison.

Man's spirit will be flesh-bound when found at best,
But uncumberèd: meadow-down is not distressed
　　For a rainbow footing it nor he for his bónes rísen.

dare-gale] storm-defying
scanted in] reduced to
bone-house] i.e. the body
aloft on turf] a piece of turf with clover was traditionally placed within skylarks' cages (which
　　were hung up 'aloft')

43

Parrot

STEVIE SMITH

The old sick green parrot
High in a dingy cage
Sick with malevolent rage
Beadily glutted his furious eye
On the old dark
Chimneys of Noel Park

Far from his jungle green
Over the seas he came
To the yellow skies, to the dripping rain,
To the night of his despair.
And the pavements of his street
Are shining beneath the lamp
With a beauty that's not for one
Born under a tropic sun.

He has croup. His feathered chest
Knows no minute of rest.
High on his perch he sits
And coughs and spits,
Waiting for death to come.
Pray heaven it won't be long.

Noel Park] a North London garden suburb
croup] a disease of the throat, causing coughing

44

At the Parrot House, Taronga Park

VIVIAN SMITH

What images could yet suggest their range
of tender colours, thick as old brocade,
or shot silk or flowers on a dress
where black and rose and lime seem to caress
the red that starts to shimmer as they fade?

Like something half-remembered from a dream
they come from places we have never seen.

They chatter and they squawk and sometimes scream.

Here the macaw clings at the rings to show
the young galahs talking as they feed
with feathers soft and pink as dawn on snow
that it too has a dry and dusky tongue.
Their murmuring embraces every need
from languid vanity to wildest greed.

In the far corner sit two smoky crones
their heads together in a kind of love.
One cleans the other's feathers while it moans.
The others seem to whisper behind fans
while noble dandies gamble in a room
asserting values everyone rejects.

A lidded eye observes, and it reflects.

The peacocks still pretend they own the yard.

For all the softness, how the beaks are hard.

Taronga Park] the zoo in Sydney, Australia
galah] (*Australian*) cockatoo

45

Eel Tail

ALICE OSWALD

sometimes you see mudfish,
those short lead lengths of eels
that hide at low tide
those roping and wagging,
preliminary, pre-world creatures, cousins of the moon,
who love blackness, aloofness,
always move under cover of the unmoon
and then as soon as you see them
                    gone
untranslatable hissed interruptions
unspeakable wide chapped lips
it's the wind again
cursing the water and when it clears

you keep looking and looking for those
underlurkers, uncontrolled little eddies,
when you lever their rooves up
they lie limbless hairless
like the bends of some huge plumbing system
sucking and sucking the marshes and
sometimes its just a smirk of ripples
and then as soon as you see them
                    gone
untranslatable hissed interruptions
unspeakable wide chapped lips
it's the wind again
bothering the reeds and when it clears

you keep looking and looking for those
backlashes waterwicks
you keep finding those sea-veins still
flowing, little cables of shadow, vanishing
dream-lines long roots of the penumbra
but they just drill down into gravel and
dwindle as quick as drips
and then as soon as you see them
                    gone
untranslatable hissed interruptions
unspeakable wide chapped lips
it's the wind again
pushing on your ears and when it clears

sometimes you see that whip-thin
tail of a waning moon start
burrowing back into blackness
and then as soon as you see her
and then as soon as you say so
                    gone

waterwicks] twisted bundles of water
penumbra] partial, graduated shadow

46

Cetacean

PETER READING

Out of Fisherman's Wharf, San Francisco, Sunday, early,
our vessel, bow to stern, some sixty-three feet,
to observe Blue Whales – and we did, off the Farallones.

They were swimming slowly, and rose at a shallow angle
(they were grey as slate with white mottling, dorsals tiny and stubby,
with broad flat heads one quarter their overall body-lengths).

They blew as soon as their heads began to break the surface.
The blows were as straight and slim as upright columns
rising to thirty feet in vertical sprays.

Then their heads disappeared underwater, and the lengthy, rolling
expanse of their backs hove into our view – about twenty feet longer
than the vessel herself.

                              And then the diminutive dorsals
showed briefly, after the blows had dispersed and the heads had
            gone under.

Then they arched their backs, then arched their tail stocks ready
            for diving.

Then the flukes were visible just before the creatures vanished,
    slipping into the deep again, at a shallow angle.

Cetacean] pertaining to the whale family
Farallones] the Farallon Islands, 30 miles offshore from San Francisco
dorsals] i.e. the small fin situated three-quarters down a whale's back
flukes] i.e. the whale's powerful tail

47

The Kraken

ALFRED, LORD TENNYSON

Below the thunders of the upper deep;
Far, far beneath in the abysmal sea,
His ancient, dreamless, uninvaded sleep
The Kraken sleepeth: faintest sunlights flee
About his shadowy sides: above him swell
Huge sponges of millennial growth and height;
And far away into the sickly light,
From many a wondrous grot and secret cell
Unnumbered and enormous polypi
Winnow with giant arms the slumbering green.
There hath he lain for ages and will lie
Battening upon huge seaworms in his sleep,
Until the latter fire shall heat the deep;
Then once by man and angels to be seen,
In roaring he shall rise and on the surface die.

Kraken] a gigantic mythical sea-monster
grot] cavern, grotto
polypi] tentacled sea-creature
Battening] feeding
the latter fire] the final flames of the apocalypse

48

Watching for Dolphins

DAVID CONSTANTINE

In the summer months on every crossing to Piraeus
One noticed that certain passengers soon rose
From seats in the packed saloon and with serious
Looks and no acknowledgement of a common purpose
Passed forward through the small door into the bows
To watch for dolphins. One saw them lose

Every other wish. Even the lovers
Turned their desires on the sea, and a fat man
Hung with equipment to photograph the occasion
Stared like a saint, through sad bi-focals; others,
Hopeless themselves, looked to the children for they
Would see dolphins if anyone would. Day after day

Or on their last opportunity all gazed
Undecided whether a flat calm were favourable
Or a sea the sun and the wind between them raised
To a likeness of dolphins. Were gulls a sign, that fell
Screeching from the sky or over an unremarkable place
Sat in a silent school? Every face

After its character implored the sea.
All, unaccustomed, wanted epiphany,
Praying the sky would clang and the abused Aegean
Reverberate with cymbal, gong and drum.
We could not imagine more prayer, and had they then
On the waves, on the climax of our longing come

Piraeus] the port-city in southern Greece
Aegean] the sea between Greece and Turkey

Smiling, snub-nosed, domed like satyrs, oh
We should have laughed and lifted the children up
Stranger to stranger, pointing how with a leap
They left their element, three or four times, centred
On grace, and heavily and warm re-entered,
Looping the keel. We should have felt them go

Further and further into the deep parts. But soon
We were among the great tankers, under their chains
In black water. We had not seen the dolphins
But woke, blinking. Eyes cast down
With no admission of disappointment the company
Dispersed and prepared to land in the city.

satyrs] in classical mythology, creatures that were part human, part beast
Looping the keel] traversing the base of the boat

49

Afternoon with Irish Cows

BILLY COLLINS

There were a few dozen who occupied the field
across the road from where we lived,
stepping all day from tuft to tuft,
their big heads down in the soft grass,
though I would sometimes pass a window
and look out to see the field suddenly empty
as if they had taken wing, flown off to another country.

Then later, I would open the blue front door,
and again the field would be full of their munching,
or they would be lying down
on the black-and-white maps of their sides,
facing in all directions, waiting for rain.
How mysterious, how patient and dumbfounded
they appeared in the long quiet of the afternoons.

But every once in a while, one of them
would let out a sound so phenomenal
that I would put down the paper
or the knife I was cutting an apple with
and walk across the road to the stone wall
to see which one of them was being torched
or pierced through the side with a long spear.

Yes, it sounded like pain until I could see
the noisy one, anchored there on all fours,
her neck outstretched, her bellowing head
laboring upward as she gave voice
to the rising, full-bodied cry
that began in the darkness of her belly
and echoed up through her bowed ribs into her
    gaping mouth.

Then I knew that she was only announcing
the large, unadulterated cowness of herself,
pouring out the ancient apologia of her kind
to all the green fields and the gray clouds,
to the limestone hills and the inlet of the blue bay,
while she regarded my head and shoulders
above the wall with one wild, shocking eye.

50

The Buck in the Snow

EDNA ST VINCENT MILLAY

White sky, over the hemlocks bowed with snow,
Saw you not at the beginning of evening the antlered buck and his doe
Standing in the apple-orchard? I saw them. I saw them suddenly go,
Tails up, with long leaps lovely and slow,
Over the stone-wall into the wood of hemlocks bowed with snow.

Now he lies here, his wild blood scalding the snow.

How strange a thing is death, bringing to his knees, bringing to his antlers
The buck in the snow.
How strange a thing--a mile away by now, it may be,
Under the heavy hemlocks that as the moments pass
Shift their loads a little, letting fall a feather of snow--
Life, looking out attentive from the eyes of the doe.

hemlocks] (*US*) fir trees
buck . . . doe] male and female deer

51

London Snow

ROBERT BRIDGES

When men were all asleep the snow came flying,
In large white flakes falling on the city brown,
Stealthily and perpetually settling and loosely lying,
   Hushing the latest traffic of the drowsy town;
Deadening, muffling, stifling its murmurs failing;
Lazily and incessantly floating down and down:
   Silently sifting and veiling road, roof and railing;
Hiding difference, making unevenness even,
Into angles and crevices softly drifting and sailing.
   All night it fell, and when full inches seven
It lay in the depth of its uncompacted lightness,
The clouds blew off from a high and frosty heaven;
   And all woke earlier for the unaccustomed brightness
Of the winter dawning, the strange unheavenly glare:
The eye marvelled—marvelled at the dazzling whiteness;
   The ear hearkened to the stillness of the solemn air;
No sound of wheel rumbling nor of foot falling,
And the busy morning cries came thin and spare.
   Then boys I heard, as they went to school, calling,
They gathered up the crystal manna to freeze
Their tongues with tasting, their hands with snowballing;
   Or rioted in a drift, plunging up to the knees;
Or peering up from under the white-mossed wonder,
'O look at the trees!' they cried, 'O look at the trees!'

crystal] i.e. formed of ice-crystals
manna] the miraculous food in the Bible, supplied by God in the desert (Exodus 16, 13–16)

With lessened load a few carts creak and blunder,
Following along the white deserted way,
A country company long dispersed asunder:
    When now already the sun, in pale display
Standing by Paul's high dome, spread forth below
His sparkling beams, and awoke the stir of the day.
    For now doors open, and war is waged with the snow;
And trains of sombre men, past tale of number,
Tread long brown paths, as toward their toil they go:
    But even for them awhile no cares encumber
Their minds diverted; the daily word is unspoken,
The daily thoughts of labour and sorrow slumber
At the sight of the beauty that greets them, for the charm they have
        broken.

Paul's high dome] the dome of St Paul's Cathedral

52

from *Crossing Brooklyn Ferry*

WALT WHITMAN

Flow on, river! flow with the flood-tide, and ebb with the ebb-tide!
Frolic on, crested and scallop-edg'd waves!
Gorgeous clouds of the sun-set! drench with your splendor me, or the
    men and women generations after me;
Cross from shore to shore, countless crowds of passengers!
Stand up, tall masts of Mannahatta!—stand up, beautiful
    hills of Brooklyn!
Throb, baffled and curious brain! throw out questions and answers!
Suspend here and everywhere, eternal float of solution!
Gaze, loving and thirsting eyes, in the house, or street, or public
    assembly!
Sound out, voices of young men! loudly and musically call me by my
    nighest name!
Live, old life! play the part that looks back on the actor or actress!
Play the old role, the role that is great or small, according as one
    makes it!

Consider, you who peruse me, whether I may not in unknown ways be
    looking upon you;
Be firm, rail over the river, to support those who lean idly, yet haste
    with the hasting current;
Fly on, sea-birds! fly sideways, or wheel in large circles high in the air;
Receive the summer sky, you water! and faithfully hold it, till all
    downcast eyes have time to take it from you;

scallop-edg'd] i.e. tipped with segmented circles like a scallop shell
Mannahatta] the original, Native American name of Manhattan (literally 'island of many hills'),
    the central island of New York
Brooklyn] the mainland New York borough

Diverge, fine spokes of light, from the shape of my head, or any
  one's head, in the sun-lit water;
Come on, ships from the lower bay! pass up or down, white-sail'd
  schooners, sloops, lighters!
Flaunt away, flags of all nations! be duly lower'd at sunset;
Burn high your fires, foundry chimneys! cast black shadows at nightfall!
  cast red and yellow light over the tops of the houses;
Appearances, now or henceforth, indicate what you are;
You necessary film, continue to envelop the soul;
About my body for me, and your body for you, be hung our divinest
  aromas;
Thrive, cities! bring your freight, bring your shows, ample and
  sufficient rivers;
Expand, being than which none else is perhaps more spiritual;
Keep your places, objects than which none else is more lasting.

schooners, sloops, lighters] varieties of small boat

53

The Storm-Wind

WILLIAM BARNES

When the swift-rolling brook, swollen deep,
   Rushes on by the alders, full speed,
And the wild-blowing winds lowly sweep
   O'er the quivering leaf and the weed,
And the willow tree writhes in each limb
Over sedge-beds that reel by the brim—

The man that is staggering by
   Holds his hat to his head by the brim;
And the girl as her hair-locks outfly,
   Puts a foot out, to keep herself trim,
And the quivering wavelings o'erspread
The small pool where the bird dips his head.

But out at my house, in the lee
   Of the nook, where the winds die away,
The light swimming airs, round the tree
   And the low-swinging ivy stem, play
So soft that a mother that's nigh
Her still cradle, may hear her babe sigh.

54

The Sea Eats the Land at Home

KOFI AWOONOR

At home the sea is in the town,
Running in and out of the cooking places,
Collecting the firewood from the hearths
And sending it back at night;
The sea eats the land at home.
It came one day at the dead of night,
Destroying the cement walls,
And carried away the fowls,
The cooking-pots and the ladles,
The sea eats the land at home;
It is a sad thing to hear the wails,
And the mourning shouts of the women,
Calling on all the gods they worship,
To protect them from the angry sea.
Aku stood outside where her cooking-pot stood,
With her two children shivering from the cold,
Her hands on her breast,
Weeping mournfully.
Her ancestors have neglected her,
Her gods have deserted her,
It was a cold Sunday morning,
The storm was raging,
Goats and fowls were struggling in the water,
The angry water of the cruel sea;
The lap-lapping of the bark water at the shore,
And above the sobs and the deep and low moans,
Was the eternal hum of the living sea.
It has taken away their belongings
Adena has lost the trinkets which
Were her dowry and her joy,
In the sea that eats the land at home,
Eats the whole land at home.

55

You will Know When You Get There

ALLEN CURNOW

Nobody comes up from the sea as late as this
in the day and the season, and nobody else goes down

the last steep kilometre, wet-metalled where
a shower passed shredding the light which keeps

pouring out of its tank in the sky, through summits,
trees, vapours thickening and thinning. Too

credibly by half celestial, the dammed
reservoir up there keeps emptying while the light lasts

over the sea, where it 'gathers the gold against
it'. The light is bits of crushed rock randomly

glinting underfoot, wetted by the short
shower, and down you go and so in its way does

the sun which gets there first. Boys, two of them,
turn campfirelit faces, a hesitancy to speak

is a hesitancy of the earth rolling back and away
behind this man going down to the sea with a bag

to pick mussels, having an arrangement with the tide,
the ocean to be shallowed three point seven metres,

one hour's light to be left, and there's the excrescent
moon sponging off the last of it. A door

slams, a heavy wave, a door, the sea-floor shudders.
Down you go alone, so late, into the surge-black
        fissure.

excrescent] growing to excess   fissure] narrow chasm

56

Written Near a Port on a Dark Evening

CHARLOTTE SMITH

Huge vapors brood above the clifted shore,
   Night on the Ocean settles, dark and mute,
Save where is heard the repercussive roar
   Of drowsy billows, on the rugged foot
Of rocks remote; or still more distant tone
   Of seamen in the anchored bark that tell
The watch relieved; or one deep voice alone
   Singing the hour, and bidding "Strike the bell."
All is black shadow, but the lucid line
   Marked by the light surf on the level sand,
Or where afar the ship-lights faintly shine
   Like wandering fairy fires, that oft on land
Mislead the Pilgrim—Such the dubious ray
That wavering Reason lends, in life's long darkling way.

clifted] cleft, divided
bark] boat, small ship
tell the watch relieved] mark the end of watchman's shift
"Strike the bell."] time was marked onboard ship with an hourly bell
darkling] i.e. in the dark

57

The Sea and the Hills

RUDYARD KIPLING

Who hath desired the Sea? -- the sight of salt water unbounded --
The heave and the halt and the hurl and the crash of the comber wind-`
  hounded?
The sleek-barrelled swell before storm, grey, foamless, enormous, and
  growing --
Stark calm on the lap of the Line or the crazy-eyed hurricane blowing --
His Sea in no showing the same his Sea and the same 'neath each
  showing:
His Sea as she slackens or thrills?
So and no otherwise -- so and no otherwise -- hillmen desire their
  Hills!

Who hath desired the Sea? -- the immense and contemptuous surges?
The shudder, the stumble, the swerve, as the star-stabbing bow-sprit
  emerges?
The orderly clouds of the Trades, the ridged, roaring sapphire
  thereunder --
Unheralded cliff-haunting flaws and the headsail's low-volleying
  thunder --
His Sea in no wonder the same his Sea and the same through each
  wonder:
His Sea as she rages or stills?
So and no otherwise -- so and no otherwise -- hillmen desire their
  Hills.

comber] a curling, breaking wave
the lap of the Line] the circuit of the Equator
bow-sprit] the projecting spar at the front of a ship
Trades] the prevalent winds forming the oceans' trade routes
cliff-haunting flaws] sudden unpredictable gusts of wind from high land

Who hath desired the Sea? Her menaces swift as her mercies?
The in-rolling walls of the fog and the silver-winged breeze that
    disperses?
The unstable mined berg going South and the calvings and groans that
    declare it --
White water half-guessed overside and the moon breaking timely to
    bare it --
His Sea as his fathers have dared -- his Sea as his children shall dare it:
His Sea as she serves him or kills?
So and no otherwise -- so and no otherwise -- hillmen desire their Hills.

Who hath desired the Sea? Her excellent loneliness rather
Than forecourts of kings, and her outermost pits than the streets
    where men gather
Inland, among dust, under trees -- inland where the slayer may slay
    him --
Inland, out of reach of her arms, and the bosom whereon he must lay
    him
His Sea from the first that betrayed -- at the last that shall never betray
    him:
His Sea that his being fulfils?
So and no otherwise -- so and no otherwise -- hillmen desire their Hills.

mined berg] an iceberg melting from below (and therefore upending)
calvings] large fragments that break from larger icebergs
White water] the foam signalling shallows

58

Blessing

IMTIAZ DHARKER

The skin cracks like a pod.
There never is enough water.

Imagine the drip of it,
the small splash, echo
in a tin mug,
the voice of a kindly god.

Sometimes, the sudden rush
of fortune. The municipal pipe bursts,
silver crashes to the ground
and the flow has found
a roar of tongues. From the huts,
a congregation: every man woman
child for streets around
butts in, with pots,
brass, copper, aluminium,
plastic buckets,
frantic hands,

and naked children
screaming in the liquid sun,
their highlights polished to perfection,
flashing light,
as the blessing sings
over their small bones.

59

The Stars Go Over the Lonely Ocean

ROBINSON JEFFERS

Unhappy about some far off things
That are not my affair, wandering
Along the coast and up the lean ridges,
I saw in the evening
The stars go over the lonely ocean,
And a black-maned wild boar
Plowing with his snout on Mal Paso Mountain.

The old monster snuffled, "Here are sweet roots,
Fat grubs, slick beetles and sprouted acorns.
The best nation in Europe has fallen,
And that is Finland,

But the stars go over the lonely ocean,"
The old black-bristled boar,
Tearing the sod on Mal Paso Mountain.

"The world's in a bad way, my man,
And bound to be worse before it mends;
Better lie up in the mountain here
Four or five centuries,
While the stars go over the lonely ocean,"
Said the old father of wild pigs,
Plowing the fallow on Mal Paso Mountain.

"Keep clear of the dupes that talk democracy
And the dogs that talk revolution,
Drunk with talk, liars and believers.
I believe in my tusks.
Long live freedom and damn the ideologies,"
Said the gamey black-maned wild boar
Tusking the turf on Mal Paso Mountain.

Mal Paso Mountain] a South American mountain range   Tearing the sod] breaking up the soil

Part 3

Travel, Migration, and Society

60

Excelsior

HENRY WADSWORTH LONGFELLOW

The shades of night were falling fast,
As through an Alpine village passed
A youth, who bore, 'mid snow and ice,
A banner with the strange device,
    Excelsior!

His brow was sad; his eye beneath,
Flashed like a falchion from its sheath,
And like a silver clarion rung
The accents of that unknown tongue,
    Excelsior!

In happy homes he saw the light
Of household fires gleam warm and bright;
Above, the spectral glaciers shone,
And from his lips escaped a groan,
    Excelsior!

"Try not the Pass!" the old man said;
"Dark lowers the tempest overhead,
The roaring torrent is deep and wide!"
And loud that clarion voice replied,
    Excelsior!

Excelsior] (*Latin*) higher
Alpine] i.e. in the Alps, the central mountain range of Europe
falchion] curved sword
lowers] (pronounced to rhyme with *hours*) hovers threateningly

"Oh, stay," the maiden said, "and rest
Thy weary head upon this breast!"
A tear stood in his bright blue eye,
But still he answered, with a sigh,
    Excelsior!

"Beware the pine-tree's withered branch!
Beware the awful avalanche!"
This was the peasant's last Good-night,
A voice replied, far up the height,
    Excelsior!

At break of day, as heavenward
The pious monks of Saint Bernard
Uttered the oft-repeated prayer,
A voice cried through the startled air,
    Excelsior!

A traveller, by the faithful hound,
Half-buried in the snow was found,
Still grasping in his hand of ice
That banner with the strange device,
    Excelsior!

There, in the twilight cold and gray,
Lifeless, but beautiful, he lay,
And from the sky, serene and far,
A voice fell, like a falling star,
    Excelsior!

Saint Bernard] the medieval monastery named after its founder, and since responsible for local
   safety
faithful hound] i.e. one of the so-called St Bernard dogs trained to locate travellers lost in the snow

61

The Mountain

ELIZABETH BISHOP

At evening, something behind me.
I start for a second, I blench,
or staggeringly halt and burn.
I do not know my age.

In the morning it is different.
An open book confronts me,
too close to read in comfort.
Tell me how old I am.

And then the valleys stuff
impenetrable mists
like cotton in my ears.
I do not know my age.

I do not mean to complain.
They say it is my fault.
Nobody tells me anything.
Tell me how old I am.

The deepest demarcations
can slowly spread and fade
like any blue tattoo.
I do not know my age.

Shadows fall down, lights climb.
Clambering lights, oh children!
you never stay long enough.
Tell me how old I am.

Stone wings have sifted here
with feather hardening feather.
The claws are lost somewhere.
I do not know my age.

62

The Road

NANCY FOTHERINGHAM CATO

I made the rising moon go back
behind the shouldering hill,
I raced along the eastern track
till time itself stood still.

The stars swarmed on behind the trees,
but I sped fast at they,
I could have made the sun arise,
and night turn back to day.

And like a long black carpet
behind the wheels, the night
unrolled across the countryside,
but all ahead was bright.

The fence-posts whizzed along wires
like days that fly too fast,
and telephone poles loomed up like years
and slipped into the past.

And light and movement, sky and road
and life and time were one,
while through the night I rushed and sped,
I drove towards the sun.

63

The Instant of My Death

SARAH JACKSON

The bus was crammed and the fat man rubbed against my leg like
        a damp cat
while you read *The Jataka Tales* three rows from the back

and we all stumbled on; wheels and hours grinding, tripping
as Spiti rose up around us, sky propped open by its peaks.

I traced the rockline on the window with my finger,
counted cows and gompas, felt my eyes glaze over

until we reached Gramphoo. There, where the road divided,
I saw a thin boy in red flannel squat between two dhabas;

a black-eyed bean, slipped-in between two crags, he was so small
that I almost missed him, until he turned, gap-toothed, and shot me

with a toy gun. And a piece of me stopped then, though the bus
        moved on,
and the fat man beside me cracked open an apple with his thumb.

The Jataka Tales] the ancient Buddhist epic
Spiti . . . Gramphoo] the Spiti Valley, in a mountainous range of the Himalayas, India, and
   a neighbouring district
gompas] Tibetan temples, or shrines
dhabas] roadside restaurant huts

64

The Bus

ARUN KOLATKAR

the tarpaulin flaps are buttoned down
on the windows of the state transport bus.
all the way up to jejuri.

a cold wind keeps whipping
and slapping a corner of tarpaulin at your elbow.

you look down to the roaring road.
you search for the signs of daybreak in what little light spills out of bus.

your own divided face in the pair of glasses
on an old man's nose
is all the countryside you get to see.

you seem to move continually forward.
toward a destination
just beyond the castemark beyond his eyebrows.

outside, the sun has risen quietly
it aims through an eyelet in the tarpaulin.
and shoots at the old man's glasses.

a sawed off sunbeam comes to rest gently against the driver's right
    temple.
the bus seems to change direction.

at the end of bumpy ride with your own face on the either side
when you get off the bus.

you dont step inside the old man's head.

jejuri] Jejuri, the city in Pune, India
castemark] manifestation of caste, or racial distinction

65

At the Bus Station

JULIUS CHINGONO

When you arrive
at the bus station
pull down your tie
or remove the tie
to prevent strangulation.
During the fight
to board the bus,
unfasten all buttons
of the shirt and jacket
to avoid losing the buttons.
During the battle
to gain entry
to the bus,
tighten both shoelaces
for, when you are hauled
into the bus,
you hang in the air
and the shoes may come off,
tighten your belt
to avoid being undressed
during the scrambling
at the door,
remove your spectacles
and hold tight to someone
until you are in the bus.
During the climb
pay no attention to human sounds,
also bear in mind
words lose meaning
until you are inside the bus.

66

These are the Times We Live in

IMTIAZ DHARKER → assumptions made

You hand over your passport. He →
looks at your face and starts →
reading you backwards from the last page.

You could be offended,
but in the end, you decide
it makes as much sense
as anything else,
given the times we live in.

You shrink to the size
of the book in his hand.
You can see his mind working:
Keep an eye on that name.
It contains a Z, and it just moved house.
The birthmark shifted recently
to another arm or leg.
Nothing is quite the same
as it should be.
But what do you expect?
It's a sign of the times we live in.

In front of you,
he flicks to the photograph,
and looks at you suspiciously.

That's when you really have to laugh.
While you were flying,
up in the air
they changed your chin
and redid your hair.

matronly, violent? / rough

They scrubbed out your mouth   *No cut off, Pendulous, dual verb, rhyme*
and rubbed out your eyes.
They made you over completely.

And all that's left is his look of surprise,
because you don't match your photograph.
Even that is coming apart.   → *significance, image invalid*

no full stop,
enjambment
emphasise ↙
the 'But',
the sting,
the meaning

The pieces are there
But they missed out your heart.

Half your face splits away,
drifts on to the page of a newspaper
that's dated today.

It rustles as it lands.   → *Anticlimax.*
                    ↳

67

The Border Builder

CAROL RUMENS

No sooner had one come down
    Than he began building again.
My bricks, O my genuine bricks
    Made of my genuine blood!
What would we be without borders?
    So which one are you? he said
And stuck out his hand to me.
    Birth certificate? Passport?
Which side are you on, which side?
    Merrily he unrolled
Starry dendrons of wire
    To give his wall ears and eyes.
Qualifications? he said.
    Residence permit? Tattoo?
Which colour are you, which colour?
    No colour, he said, no good.
He took my only passport,
    He slammed it down on the wire.
My hand, O my genuine hand!
    This is a border, he said.
A border likes blood. Which side's
    Your bloody hand on, which side?

dendrons] crystalline branches ('Starry' because of the barbs in barbed wire)

68

The Migrant

A.L. HENDRIKS

She could not remember anything about the voyage,
Her country of origin, or if someone had paid for the passage:
Of such she had no recollection.

She was sure only that she had travelled;
Without doubt had been made welcome.

For a while she believed she was home,
Rooted and securely settled,
Until it was broken to her
That in fact she was merely in transit
Bound for some other destination,
Committed to continue elsewhere.

This slow realization sharpened,
She formed plans to postpone her departure
Not observing her movement en route to the exit.

When she did, it was piteous how, saddened,
She went appreciably closer towards it.
Eventually facing the inescapable
She began reading travel brochures,
(Gaudy, competitive, plentiful)
Spent time considering the onward journey,
Studied a new language,
Stuffed her bosom with strange currency,
Nevertheless dreading the boarding announcements.

We watch her go through
The gate for *Embarking Passengers Only*,
Fearful and unutterably lonely,
Finger our own documents,
Shuffle forward in the queue.

en route] (French) on the way   in transit] (Latin: in transitu) on a continuing journey

69

The White House

'all men are created equal'

USA power

CLAUDE MCKAY

civil rights

Your door is shut against my tightened face,
And I am sharp as steel with discontent;
But I possess the courage and the grace
To bear my anger proudly and unbent.
The pavement slabs burn loose beneath my feet,
A chafing savage, down the decent street;
And passion rends my vitals as I pass,
Where boldly shines your shuttered door of glass.
Oh, I must search for wisdom every hour,
Deep in my wrathful bosom sore and raw,
And find in it the superhuman power
To hold me to the letter of your law!
Oh, I must keep my heart inviolate
Against the potent poison of your hate.

70

The Enemies

ELIZABETH JENNINGS

Last night they came across the river and
Entered the city. Women were awake
With lights and food. They entertained the band,
Not asking what the men had come to take
Or what strange tongue they spoke
Or why they came so suddenly through the land.

Now in the morning all the town is filled
With stories of the swift and dark invasion;
The women say that not one stranger told
A reason for his coming. The intrusion
Was not for devastation:
Peace is apparent still on hearth and field.

Yet all the city is a haunted place.
Man meeting man speaks cautiously. Old friends
Close up the candid looks upon their face.
There is no warmth in hands accepting hands;
Each ponders, 'Better hide myself in case
Those strangers have set up their homes in minds
I used to walk in. Better draw the blinds
Even if the strangers haunt in my own house.'

71

Who in One Lifetime

MURIEL RUKEYSER

Who in one lifetime sees all causes lost,
Herself dismayed and helpless, cities down,
Love made monotonous fear and the sad-faced
Inexorable armies and the falling plane,
Has sickness, sickness. Introspective and whole.
She knows how several madnesses are born,
Seeing the integrated never fighting well,
The flesh too vulnerable, the eyes tear-torn.

She finds a pre-surrender on all sides:
Treaty before the war, ritual impatience turn
The camps of ambush to chambers of imagery.
She holds belief in the world, she stays and hides
Life in her own defeat, stands, though her whole world burn
A childless goddess of fertility.

72

The Hour is Come

LOUISA LAWSON

How did she fight? She fought well.
How did she light? Ah, she fell.
Why did she fall? God, who knows all,
Only can tell.

Those she was fighting for – they
Surely would go to her? Nay!
What of her pain! Theirs is the gain.
Ever the way.

Will they not help her to rise
If there is death in her eyes?
Can you not see? She made them free.
What if she dies?

Can we not help her? Oh, no!
In her good fight it is so
That all who work never must shirk
Suff'ring and woe.

But she'll not ever lie down –
On her head, in the dust, is a crown
Jewelled and bright, under whose light
She'll rise alone.

73

At the "Capitol"

KEVIN HALLIGAN

The spy relaxes with the morning paper
Under the metal awning
On a red plastic chair. His shirt is unbuttoned.

Daily he takes up the same position,
Aloof from the mix of foreigners,
The roar of the rush hour at his back.

Like a spy in a film or a comic strip,
Every so often he raises his eyes
And lifts the long spoon in his *café crème*.

When friends or acquaintances rise
And kick-start their bikes,
He waves and returns to the headlines.

We ignore him; indeed, we take him for granted
Under the echoing awning
That throws our voices in his direction.

74

Boxes

SAMPURNA CHATTARJI

Her balcony bears an orchid smuggled in a duffle bag
from Singapore. Its roots cling to air. For two hours
every morning the harsh October sun turns tender
at its leaves. Nine steps from door to balcony and
already she is a giant insect fretting in a jar.

On one side of her one-room home, a stove, where she
cooks dal in an iron pan. The smell of food is good.
Through the window bars the sing-song of voices high
then low in steady arcs. With his back to the wall,
a husband, and a giant stack of quilts, threatening to fall.

Sleeping room only, a note on the door should have read,
readying you for cramp. Fall in and kick off your shoes.
Right-angled to this corridor with a bed, trains make tracks
to unfamiliar sounding places. Unhidden by her curtains,
two giant black pigs lie dead, or asleep, on a dump.

Every day the city grows taller, trampling underfoot
students wives lovers babies. The boxes grow smaller.
The sea becomes a distant memory of lashing wave
and neon, siren to seven islands, once. The sky strides
inland on giant stilts, unstoppable, shutting out the light.

siren] a mythological monster who lured sailors onto rocks by her beautiful singing

75

The Capital

W.H. AUDEN

Quarter of pleasures where the rich are always waiting,
Waiting expensively for miracles to happen,
O little restaurant where the lovers eat each other,
Café where exiles have established a malicious village;

You with your charm and your apparatus have abolished
The strictness of winter and the spring's compulsion;
Far from your lights the outraged punitive father,
The dullness of mere obedience here is apparent.

Yet with orchestras and glances, O, you betray us
To belief in our infinite powers; and the innocent
Unobservant offender falls in a moment
Victim to the heart's invisible furies.

In unlighted streets you hide away the appalling;
Factories where lives are made for a temporary use
Like collars or chairs, rooms where the lonely are battered
Slowly like pebbles into fortuitous shapes.

But the sky you illumine, your glow is visible far
Into the dark countryside, the enormous, the frozen,
Where, hinting at the forbidden like a wicked uncle,
Night after night to the farmer's children you beckon.

collars] i.e. the detachable, disposable collars once worn with shirts

76

The Cry of the Children

ELIZABETH BARRETT BROWNING

'φεῦ, φεῦ, τί προσδέρκεσθέ μ 'ὄμμασιν, τέκνα.' *MEDEA*

Do ye hear the children weeping, O my brothers,
    Ere the sorrow comes with years?
They are leaning their young heads against their mothers,—
    And *that* cannot stop their tears.
The young lambs are bleating in the meadows;
  The young birds are chirping in the nest;
The young fawns are playing with the shadows;
  The young flowers are blowing toward the west—
But the young, young children, O my brothers,
    They are weeping bitterly!—
They are weeping in the playtime of the others,
    In the country of the free.

Do you question the young children in the sorrow,
    Why their tears are falling so?—
The old man may weep for his to-morrow
    Which is lost in Long Ago—
The old tree is leafless in the forest—
  The old year is ending in the frost—
The old wound, if stricken, is the sorest—
  The old hope is hardest to be lost:
But the young, young children, O my brothers,
    Do you ask them why they stand
Weeping sore before the bosoms of their mothers,
    In our happy Fatherland?

Epigraph] 'Alas, alas, why do you gaze at me with your eyes, my children', from Euripides,
    Medea (c. 430 BC), whose heroine kills her own children in revenge on her unfaithful husband

They look up with their pale and sunken faces,
    And their looks are sad to see,
For the man's grief abhorrent, draws and presses
    Down the cheeks of infancy—
'Your old earth,' they say, 'is very dreary;'
    'Our young feet,' they say, 'are very weak!
Few paces have we taken, yet are weary—
    Our grave-rest is very far to seek.
Ask the old why they weep, and not the children,
    For the outside earth is cold,—
And we young ones stand without, in our bewildering,
    And the graves are for the old.

77

an afternoon nap

ARTHUR YAP

the ambitious mother across the road
is at it again. proclaiming her goodness
she beats the boy. shouting out his wrongs, with raps
she begins with his mediocre report-book grades.

she strikes chords for the afternoon piano lesson,
her voice stridently imitates 2nd. lang. tuition,
all the while circling the cowering boy
in a manner apt for the most strenuous p.e. ploy.

swift are all her contorted movements,
ape for every need; no soft gradient
of a consonant-vowel figure, she lumbers
& shrieks, a hit for every 2 notes missed.

his tears are dear. each monday,
wednesday, friday, miss low & madam lim
appear & take away $90 from the kitty
leaving him an adagio, clause analysis, little
pocket-money.

the embittered boy across the road
is at it again. proclaiming his bewilderment
he yells at her. shouting out her wrongs, with tears
he begins with her expensive taste for education.

a consonant-vowel figure] a linguistic diagram
adagio] musical instruction to indicate a slow performance
clause analysis] the exercise of parsing a sentence

78

Plaits

ELIZABETH SMITHER

I had two plaits: one thick
an anaconda plait and the other
more like a thin grass snake.

My parting was on one side
a harvest, a rich waterfall
and a thin trickling river

but they were companionably joined
and tied with a wide ribbon
whose loops and bows were equal.

The weak and the strong
were strong together, the raised segments
of hair, a wide and thin muscle

a lesson that hung down my back
so though I could not see justice
I could feel how it was distributed.

79

Shirt

ROBERT PINSKY

The back, the yoke, the yardage. Lapped seams,
The nearly invisible stitches along the collar
Turned in a sweatshop by Koreans or Malaysians

Gossiping over tea and noodles on their break
Or talking money or politics while one fitted
This armpiece with its overseam to the band

Of cuff I button at my wrist. The presser, the cutter,
The wringer, the mangle. The needle, the union,
The treadle, the bobbin. The code. The infamous blaze

At the Triangle Factory in nineteen-eleven.
One hundred and forty-six died in the flames
On the ninth floor, no hydrants, no fire escapes –

The witness in a building across the street
Who watched how a young man helped a girl to step
up to the windowsill, then held her out

Away from the masonry wall and let her drop.
And then another. As if he were helping them up
To enter a streetcar, and not eternity.

A third before he dropped her put her arms
Around his neck and kissed him, Then he held
Her into space, and dropped her. Almost at once

Triangle Factory in nineteen-eleven] the notorious ('infamous') fire at the Triangle
Shirtwaist Factory in New York in March 1911

He stepped to the sill himself, his jacket flared
And fluttered up from his shirt as he came down,
Air filling up the legs of his gray trousers –

Like Hart Crane's Bedlamite, "shrill shirt ballooning".
Wonderful how the pattern matches perfectly
Across the placket and over the twin bar-tacked

Corners of both pockets, like a strict rhyme
Or a major chord. Prints, plaids, checks,
Houndstooth, Tattersall, Madras. The clan tartans

Invented by mill-owners inspired by the hoax of Ossian,
To control their savage Scottish workers, tamed
By a fabricated heraldry: MacGregor,

Bailey, MacMartin. The kilt, devised for workers
To wear among the dusty clattering looms.
Weavers, carders, spinners. The loader,

The docker, the navvy. The planter, the picker, the sorter
Sweating at her machine in a litter of cotton
As slaves in calico headrags sweated in fields:

George Herbert, your descendant is a Black
Lady in South Carolina, her name is Irma
And she inspected my shirt. Its color and fit

And feel and its clean smell have satisfied
Both her and me. We have culled its cost and quality
Down to the buttons of simulated bone,

The buttonholes, the sizing, the facing, the characters
Printed in black on neckband and tail. The shape,
The label, the labor, the color, the shade. The shirt.

Hart Crane's Bedlamite] the American Hart Crane's poem 'To Brooklyn Bridge' (1930):
   'A bedlamite [= madman] speeds to thy parapets, | Tilting there momently, shrill shirt ballooning'.
Prints . . . Madras] types of fabric pattern
the hoax of Ossian] a notorious eighteenth-century literary forgery, written and published by James
   Macpherson, but purporting to be his translation of an ancient Gaelic epic
George Herbert] Welsh metaphysical poet (1593–1633)

80

The Song of the Shirt

THOMAS HOOD

With fingers weary and worn,
  With eyelids heavy and red,
A woman sat in unwomanly rags,
  Plying her needle and thread—
    Stitch! stitch! stitch!
In poverty, hunger, and dirt,
  And still with a voice of dolorous pitch
She sang the "Song of the Shirt!"

"Work—work—work
  Till the brain begins to swim;
Work—work—work
  Till the eyes are heavy and dim.
Seam, and gusset, and band,
  Band, and gusset, and seam,
Till over the buttons I fall asleep,
  And sew them on in a dream!

"Oh, Men, with Sisters dear!
  Oh, Men, with Mothers and Wives!
It is not linen you 're wearing out,
  But human creatures' lives!
    Stitch—stitch—stitch,
  In poverty, hunger, and dirt,
Sewing at once, with a double thread,
  A Shroud as well as a Shirt.

"But why do I talk of Death?
  That Phantom of grisly bone,
I hardly fear his terrible shape,
  It seems so like my own—
It seems so like my own,
  Because of the fasts I keep;
Oh, God! that bread should be so dear,
  And flesh and blood so cheap!

"Work—work—work,
  My labor never flags;
And what are its wages? A bed of straw,
  A crust of bread—and rags.
That shatter'd roof—and this naked floor—
  A table—a broken chair—
And a wall so blank, my shadow I thank
  For sometimes falling there.

"Work—work—work!
From weary chime to chime,
  Work—work—work,
As prisoners work for crime!
  Band, and gusset, and seam,
  Seam, and gusset, and band,
Till the heart is sick, and the brain benumb'd,
  As well as the weary hand.

"Work—work—work,
In the dull December light,
  And work—work—work,
When the weather is warm and bright,
While underneath the eaves
  The brooding swallows cling
As if to show me their sunny backs
  And twit me with the spring.

twit] taunt

"Oh! but to breathe the breath
Of the cowslip and primrose sweet,
  With the sky above my head,
And the grass beneath my feet,
For only one short hour
  To feel as I used to feel,
Before I knew the woes of want
  And the walk that costs a meal,

"Oh, but for one short hour!
  A respite however brief!
No blessed leisure for Love or Hope,
  But only time for Grief!
A little weeping would ease my heart,
  But in their briny bed
My tears must stop, for every drop
  Hinders needle and thread!"

With fingers weary and worn,
  With eyelids heavy and red
A woman sat in unwomanly rags,
  Plying her needle and thread—
Stitch! stitch! stitch!
  In poverty, hunger, and dirt,
And still with a voice of dolorous pitch,
Would that its tone could reach the Rich!
  She sang this " Song of the Shirt!"

the walk that costs a meal] i.e. the cost in unpaid wages of taking time off work
briny bed] i.e. the eyes (where salty tears begin)

81

Children of Wealth

ELIZABETH DARYUSH

Children of wealth in your warm nursery,
Set in the cushioned window-seat to watch
The volleying snow, guarded invisibly
By the clear double pane through which no touch
Untimely penetrates, you cannot tell
What winter means; its cruel truths to you
Are only sound and sight; your citadel
Is safe from feeling, and from knowledge too.

Go down, go out to elemental wrong,
Waste your too round limbs, tan your skin too white;
The glass of comfort, ignorance, seems strong
Today, and yet perhaps this very night

You'll wake to horror's wrecking fire—your home
Is wired within for this, in every room.

82

from *The Complaints of Poverty*

NICHOLAS JAMES

When winter's rage upon the cottage falls,
And the wind rushes through the gaping walls,
When ninepence must their daily wants supply,
With hunger pinched and cold, the children cry;
The gathered sticks but little warmth afford,
And half-supplied the platter meets the board.
Returned at night, if wholesome viands fail,
He from the pipe extracts a smoky meal:
And when, to gather strength and still his woes,
He seeks his last redress in soft repose,
The tattered blanket, erst the fleas' retreat,
Denies his shiv'ring limbs sufficient heat;
Teased with the squalling babes' nocturnal cries,
He restless on the dusty pillow lies.
    But when pale sickness wounds with direful blow,
Words but imperfectly his mis'ry show;
Unskilful how to treat the fierce disease,
Well-meaning ignorance curtails our days.
In a dark room and miserable bed
Together lie the living and the dead.
Oh shocking scene! Fate sweeps whole tribes away,
And frees the parish of th' reluctant pay!
Where's the physician now, whom heav'n ordains
Fate to arrest, and check corroding pains?
Or he's detained by those of high degree,
Or won't prescribe without a golden fee.

---

smoky meal] i.e. tobacco (with the sense of an insubstantial and transient one)
erst the fleas' retreat] previously occupied by fleas
frees the parish of th' reluctant pay] relieves the parish authorities of its grudging welfare payments

But should old age bring on its rev'rend hoar,
When strength decayed admits his toil no more,
He begs itinerant, with halting pace,
And, mournful, tells his melancholy case,
With meagre cheek and formidable beard,
A tattered dress of various rags prepared.
　　Base covetise, who wants the soul to give,
Directs the road where richer neighbours live;
And pride, unmindful of its parent dust,
Scares with the dungeon and the whipping-post.

its rev'rend hoar] venerable appearance
Base covetise, who wants the soul to give] Mean-spirited wealthy people, who are incapable of
　　understanding charity

83

To a Millionaire

A.R.D. FAIRBURN

Lord of our world, take off your velvet
mask. Remove your gentle glove, disclose
the claw-like hand, the dried blood under the nails,
the murder print that never shows.

We have spotted your guilt before the final
bloodstained page of our modern super-thriller;
ignoring the views of the bum police detective
we have identified the killer
We have explored your paradise
in the unpacific ocean, where many drown;
we know the zoology of your coral island;
we have counted the skulls beneath your town.

Tended by tight-lipped servants, muse
on the day the rabble will spit on your polished floor,
yourself forgotten like foul weather, groomed
by the worm, your patient servitor.

There will be little of your estate
after the notary Clay has proved your will;
your assets will melt in the great slump, and time's
invisible violence do you ill.

You have forgotten the diver dead
of a bad heart who groped for your wife's pearls.
Her diamonds shine like water sprinkled on bought
flowers, or the sweat of factory girls.

bum] ineffective
diver] i.e. one who dives to the seabed to gather pearls

Your opulent curtains woven of blood
lend a sweet charnel fragrance to your room.
Under your rich carpet are bones buried
that shall speak up at crack of doom.

You cover your pits with grass, ascribe
our broken limbs to Providence; you advise
gentleness and restraint, you counsel prayer,
for when men pray they shut their eyes.
What is your world but a dark glass
that is thronged with images of its own disruption,
your soul but a facing mirror that reflects back
the accurate pattern of corruption?

Two mirrors in rigid dialectic
display the secular process of your life,
leading through infinite recession to nothingness
yourself, your world of strife.

cover your pits with grass] conceal the traps you have laid
Providence] God's supervising plan

84

Rich and Poor or, Saint and Sinner

THOMAS LOVE PEACOCK

The poor man's sins are glaring;
In the face of ghostly warning
  He is caught in the fact
  Of an overt act—
Buying greens on Sunday morning.

The rich man's sins are hidden
In the pomp of wealth and station;
  And escape the sight
  Of the children of light,
Who are wise in their generation.

The rich man has a kitchen,
And cooks to dress his dinner;
  The poor who would roast
  To the baker's must post,
And thus becomes a sinner.

The rich man has a cellar,
And a ready butler by him;
  The poor must steer
  For his pint of beer
Where the saint can't choose but spy him.

children of light] enlightened authorities (see Luke 16, 8: 'for the children of this world are in their
  generation wiser than the children of light')
dress] prepare
The poor who would roast | To the baker's must post] poor people, lacking their own means to cook
  their food, must commission a tradesman to do so – and thus fall foul of the commandment
  against working on the Sabbath

The rich man's painted windows
Hide the concerts of the quality;
  The poor can but share
  A crack'd fiddle in the air,
Which offends all sound morality.

The rich man is invisible
In the crowd of his gay society;
  But the poor man's delight
  Is a sore in the sight,
And a stench in the nose of piety.

The rich man has a carriage
Where no rude eye can flout him;
  The poor man's bane
  Is a third-class train,
With the day-light all about him.

The rich man goes out yachting
Where sanctity can't pursue him;
  The poor goes afloat
  In a fourpenny boat,
Where the bishops groan to view him.

the nose of piety] the refined sensibilities of the pious

85

A Long Journey

MUSAEMURA ZIMUNYA

Through decades that ran like rivers
endless rivers of endless woes
through pick and shovel sjambok and jail
O such a long long journey

When the motor-car came
the sledge and the ox-cart began to die
but for a while the bicycle made in Britain
was the dream of every village boy

With the arrival of the bus
the city was brought into the village
and we began to yearn for the place behind the horizons

Such a long travail it was
a long journey from bush to concrete

And now I am haunted by the cave dwelling
hidden behind eighteen ninety
threatening my new-found luxury
in this the capital city of my mother country
I fight in nightmarish vain
but my road runs and turns into dusty gravel
into over-beaten foot tracks that lead
to a plastic hut and soon to a mud-grass dwelling
threatened by wind and rain and cold

sjambok] whip (made of hide)
eighteen ninety] Zimbabwe (then Rhodesia) came under British colonial rule in 1890

We have fled from witches and wizards
on a long long road to the city
but behind the halo of tower lights
I hear the cry from human blood
and wicked bones rattling around me

We moved into the lights
but from the dark periphery behind
an almighty hand reaches for our shirts.

86

Touch and Go

STEVIE SMITH

Man is coming out of the mountains
But his tail is caught in the pass.
Why does he not free himself
Is he not an ass?

Do not be impatient with him
He is bowed with passion and fret
He is not out of the mountains
He is not half out yet.

Look at his sorrowful eyes
His torn cheeks, his brow
He lies with his head in the dust
Is there no one to help him now?

No, there is no one to help him
Let him get on with it
Cry the ancient enemies of man
As they cough and spit.

The enemies of man are like trees
They stand with the sun in their branches
Is there no one to help my creature
Where he languishes?

Ah, the delicate creature
He lies with his head in the rubble
Pray that the moment pass
And the trouble.

Look he moves, that is more than a prayer,
But he is so slow
Will he come out of the mountains?
It is touch and go.

87

First March

IVOR GURNEY

It was first marching, hardly we had settled yet
To think of England, or escaped body pain—
Flat country going leaves but small chance for
The mind to escape to any resort but its vain
Own circling greyness and stain.
First halt, second halt, and then to spoiled country again.
There were unknown kilometres to march, one must settle
To play chess or talk home-talk or think as might happen.
After three weeks of February frost few were in fettle,
Barely frostbite the most of us had escapen.
To move, then to go onward, at least to be moved.
Myself had revived and then dulled down, it was I
Who stared for body-ease at the grey sky
And watched in grind of pain the monotony
Of grit, road metal, slide underneath by.
To get there being the one way not to die.
Suddenly a road's turn brought the sweet unexpected
Balm. Snowdrops bloomed in a ruined garden neglected:
Roman the road as of Birdlip we were on the verge,
And this west country thing so from chaos to emerge.
One gracious touch the whole wilderness corrected.

Birdlip] a village in the English Cotswolds (in the 'west country' of Gloucestershire)

88

On the Day of Judgement

JONATHAN SWIFT

With a whirl of thought oppressed,
I sink from reverie to rest.
An horrid vision seized my head,
I saw the graves give up their dead.
Jove, armed with terrors, burst the skies,
And thunder roars, and light'ning flies!
Amazed, confused, its fate unknown,
The world stands trembling at his throne.
While each pale sinner hangs his head,
Jove, nodding, shook the heav'ns, and said,
'Offending race of human kind,
By nature, reason, learning, blind;
You who through frailty stepped aside,
And you who never fell—through pride;
You who in different sects have shammed,
And come to see each other damned;
(So some folks told you, but they knew
No more of Jove's designs than you);
The world's mad business now is o'er,
And I resent these pranks no more.
I to such blockheads set my wit!
I damn such fools!—Go, go, you're bit.'

Jove] the Roman king of the gods (here the Christian God)
bit] i.e. bitten; damned to torment in the jaws of hell

89

Darkness

GEORGE GORDON, LORD BYRON

I had a dream, which was not all a dream.
The bright sun was extinguish'd, and the stars
Did wander darkling in the eternal space,
Rayless, and pathless, and the icy earth
Swung blind and blackening in the moonless air;
Morn came, and went—and came, and brought no day,
And men forgot their passions in the dread
Of this their desolation; and all hearts
Were chill'd into a selfish prayer for light:
And they did live by watchfires—and the thrones,
The palaces of crowned kings—the huts,
The habitations of all things which dwell,
Were burnt for beacons; cities were consumed,
And men were gathered round their blazing homes
To look once more into each other's face;
Happy were those who dwelt within the eye
Of the volcanos, and their mountain-torch:
A fearful hope was all the world contain'd;
Forests were set on fire—but hour by hour
They fell and faded—and the crackling trunks
Extinguish'd with a crash—and all was black.
The brows of men by the despairing light
Wore an unearthly aspect, as by fits
The flashes fell upon them; some lay down
And hid their eyes and wept; and some did rest
Their chins upon their clenched hands, and smiled;
And others hurried to and fro, and fed
Their funeral piles with fuel, and looked up
With mad disquietude on the dull sky,

darkling] in the dark

The pall of a past world; and then again
With curses cast them down upon the dust,
And gnash'd their teeth and howl'd: the wild birds shriek'd,
And, terrified, did flutter on the ground,
And flap their useless wings; the wildest brutes
Came tame and tremulous; and vipers crawl'd
And twined themselves among the multitude,
Hissing, but stingless—they were slain for food:
And War, which for a moment was no more,
Did glut himself again;—a meal was bought
With blood, and each sate sullenly apart
Gorging himself in gloom: no love was left;
All earth was but one thought—and that was death,
Immediate and inglorious; and the pang
Of famine fed upon all entrails—men
Died, and their bones were tombless as their flesh;
The meagre by the meagre were devoured,
Even dogs assail'd their masters, all save one,
And he was faithful to a corse, and kept
The birds and beasts and famish'd men at bay,
Till hunger clung them, or the dropping dead
Lured their lank jaws; himself sought out no food,
But with a piteous and perpetual moan,
And a quick desolate cry, licking the hand
Which answered not with a caress—he died.
The crowd was famish'd by degrees; but two
Of an enormous city did survive,
And they were enemies; they met beside
The dying embers of an altar-place,
Where had been heap'd a mass of holy things
For an unholy usage; they raked up,
And shivering scraped with their cold skeleton hands
The feeble ashes, and their feeble breath
Blew for a little life, and made a flame
Which was a mockery; then they lifted up
Their eyes as it grew lighter, and beheld
Each other's aspects—saw, and shriek'd, and died—
Even of their mutual hideousness they died,
Unknowing who he was upon whose brow
Famine had written Fiend. The world was void,

corse] body, corpse
clung] shrivelled, caused to shrink

The populous and the powerful—was a lump,
Seasonless, herbless, treeless, manless, lifeless—
A lump of death—a chaos of hard clay.
The rivers, lakes, and ocean all stood still,
And nothing stirred within their silent depths;
Ships sailorless lay rotting on the sea,
And their masts fell down piecemeal; as they dropp'd
They slept on the abyss without a surge—
The waves were dead; the tides were in their grave,
The moon their mistress had expired before;
The winds were withered in the stagnant air,
And the clouds perish'd; Darkness had no need
Of aid from them—She was the universe.

their mistress] i.e. because the moon governs the tide

90

Song

GEORGE SZIRTES

for Helen Suzman

Nothing happens until something does.
Everything remains just as it was
And all you hear is the distant buzz
Of nothing happening till something does.

A lot of small hands in a monstrous hall
can make the air vibrate
and even shake the wall;
a voice can break a plate
or glass, and one pale feather tip
the balance on a sinking ship.

It's the very same tune that has been sung
time and again by those
whose heavy fate has hung
on the weight that they oppose,
the weight by which are crushed
the broken voices of the hushed.

But give certain people a place to stand
a lever, a fulcrum, a weight,
however small the hand,
the object however great,
it is possible to prove
that even Earth may be made to move.

Helen Suzman] (1917–2009), South African anti-apartheid campaigner
a lever . . . even Earth may be made to move] i.e. the theoretical principal asserted by the Ancient
  Greek mathematician Archimedes

Nothing happens until something does,
and hands, however small,
fill the air so the buzz
of the broken fills the hall
as levers and fulcrums shift
and the heart like a weight begins to lift.

Nothing happens until something does.
Everything remains just as it was
And all you hear is the distant buzz
Of nothing happening. Then something does.

Part 4

Love, Wisdom, and Age

91

A Complaint

WILLIAM WORDSWORTH

There is a change—and I am poor;
Your love hath been, nor long ago,
A fountain at my fond heart's door,
Whose only business was to flow;
And flow it did; not taking heed
Of its own bounty, or my need.

What happy moments did I count!
Blest was I then all bliss above!
Now, for that consecrated fount
Of murmuring, sparkling, living love,
What have I? shall I dare to tell?
A comfortless and hidden well.

A well of love—it may be deep—
I trust it is,—and never dry:
What matter? if the waters sleep
In silence and obscurity.
—Such change, and at the very door
Of my fond heart, hath made me poor.

nor long ago] i.e. and not too long ago

92

A Song of Faith Forsworn

JOHN WARREN, LORD DE TABLEY

Take back your suit.
It came when I was weary and distraught
With hunger. Could I guess the fruit you brought?
I ate in mere desire of any food,
Nibbled its edge and nowhere found it good.
Take back your suit.

Take back your love,
It is a bird poached from my neighbour's wood:
Its wings are wet with tears, its beak with blood.
'Tis a strange fowl with feathers like a crow:
Death's raven, it may be, for all we know.
Take back your love.

Take back your gifts.
False is the hand that gave them; and the mind
That planned them, as a hawk spread in the wind
To poise and snatch the trembling mouse below.
To ruin where it dares – and then to go.
Take back your gifts.

Take back your vows.
Elsewhere you trimmed and taught these lamps to burn;
You bring them stale and dim to serve my turn.
You lit those candles in another shrine,
Guttered and cold you offer them on mine.
Take back your vows.

trimmed] adjusted the wicks of candles (to burn clear)

Take back your words.
What is your love? Leaves on a woodland plain,
Where some are running and where some remain:
What is your faith? Straws on a mountain height,
Dancing like demons on Walpurgis night.
Take back your words.

Take back your lies.
Have them again: they wore a rainbow face,
Hollow with sin and leprous with disgrace;
Their tongue was like a mellow turret bell
To toll hearts burning into wide-lipped hell.
Take back your lies.

Take back your kiss.
Shall I be meek, and lend my lips again
To let this adder daub them with his stain?
Shall I turn cheek to answer, when I hate?
You kiss like Judas in the garden gate!
Take back your kiss.

Take back delight,
A paper boat launched on a heaving pool
To please a child, and folded by a fool;
The wild elms roared: it sailed – a yard or more.
Out went our ship but never came to shore.
Take back delight.

Take back your wreath.
Has it done service on a fairer brow?
Fresh, was it folded round her bosom snow?
Her cast-off weed my breast will never wear:
Your word is 'love me.' My reply 'despair!'
Take back your wreath.

Walpurgis night] a European spring festival associated with sorcerers and witches
Judas in the garden gate] i.e. the disciple who betrayed Jesus with a kiss in the Garden of
  Gethsemane

93

The Forsaken Wife

[handwritten annotations: hurt; 1722; 16 yr engagement; woman scorned]

ELIZABETH THOMAS ('CORINNA')

[handwritten annotation: Rhyme scheme, undermining?, thought thru — Passive aggressive, planned]

Methinks 'tis strange you can't afford
One pitying look, one parting word.
Humanity claims this as its due,
But what's humanity to you?

   Cruel man! I am not blind;
Your infidelity I find.
Your want of love my ruin shows,
My broken heart, your broken vows.
Yet maugre all your rigid hate
I will be true in spite of fate,
And one preëminence I'll claim,
To be forever still the same.

   Show me a man that dare be true,
That dares to suffer what I do,
That can forever sigh unheard,
And ever love without regard,
I will then own your prior claim
To love, to honour and to fame,
But till that time, my dear, adieu.
I yet superior am to you.

want] lack
maugre] despite

94

Farewell, Ungrateful Traitor

JOHN DRYDEN

Farewell, ungrateful traitor,
Farewell, my perjured swain,
Let never injured creature
Believe a man again.
The pleasure of possessing
Surpasses all expressing,
But 'tis too short a blessing,
And love too long a pain.

'Tis easy to deceive us
In pity of your pain,
But when we love you leave us
To rail at you in vain.
Before we have descried it
There is no bliss beside it,
But she that once has tried it
Will never love again.

The passion you pretended
Was only to obtain,
But when the charm is ended
The charmer you disdain.
Your love by ours we measure
Till we have lost our treasure,
But dying is a pleasure,
When living is a pain.

swain] wooer, lover
descried] become aware of, discovered

95

After

PHILIP BOURKE MARSTON

I

A little time for laughter,
  A little time to sing,
  A little time to kiss and cling,
And no more kissing after.

II

A little while for scheming
  Love's unperfected schemes;
  A little time for golden dreams,
Then no more any dreaming.

III

A little while 'twas given
  To me to have thy love;
  Now, like a ghost, alone I move
About a ruined heaven.

IV

A little time for speaking,
  Things sweet to say and hear;
  A time to seek, and find thee near,
Then no more any seeking.

V

A little time for saying
 Words the heart breaks to say;
 A short, sharp time wherein to pray,
Then no more need for praying;

VI

But long, long years to weep in,
 And comprehend the whole
 Great grief that desolates the soul,
And eternity to sleep in.

96

A Leave-Taking

ALGERNON CHARLES SWINBURNE

Let us go hence, my songs; she will not hear.
Let us go hence together without fear;
Keep silence now, for singing-time is over,
And over all old things and all things dear.
She loves not you nor me as all we love her.
Yea, though we sang as angels in her ear,
  She would not hear.

Let us rise up and part; she will not know.
Let us go seaward as the great winds go,
Full of blown sand and foam; what help is here?
There is no help, for all these things are so,
And all the world is bitter as a tear.
And how these things are, though ye strove to show,
  She would not know.

Let us go home and hence; she will not weep.
We gave love many dreams and days to keep,
Flowers without scent, and fruits that would not grow,
Saying 'If thou wilt, thrust in thy sickle and reap.'
All is reaped now; no grass is left to mow;
And we that sowed, though all we fell on sleep,
  She would not weep.

Let us go hence and rest; she will not love.
She shall not hear us if we sing hereof,
Nor see love's ways, how sore they are and steep.
Come hence, let be, lie still; it is enough.
Love is a barren sea, bitter and deep;
And though she saw all heaven in flower above,
  She would not love.

Let us give up, go down; she will not care.
Though all the stars made gold of all the air,
And the sea moving saw before it move
One moon-flower making all the foam-flowers fair;
Though all those waves went over us, and drove
Deep down the stifling lips and drowning hair,
        She would not care.

Let us go hence, go hence; she will not see.
Sing all once more together; surely she,
She too, remembering days and words that were,
Will turn a little toward us, sighing; but we,
We are hence, we are gone, as though we had not been there.
Nay, and though all men seeing had pity on me,
        She would not see.

97

When We Two Parted

GEORGE GORDON, LORD BYRON

When we two parted
    In silence and tears,
Half broken-hearted
    To sever for years,
Pale grew thy cheek and cold,
    Colder thy kiss;
Truly that hour foretold
    Sorrow to this.

The dew of the morning
    Sunk chill on my brow—
It felt like the warning
    Of what I feel now.
Thy vows are all broken,
    And light is thy fame;
I hear thy name spoken,
    And share in its shame.

They name thee before me,
    A knell to mine ear;
A shudder comes o'er me—
    Why wert thou so dear?
They know not I knew thee,
    Who knew thee too well:—
Long, long shall I rue thee,
    Too deeply to tell.

In secret we met—
    In silence I grieve,
That thy heart could forget,
    Thy spirit deceive.
If I should meet thee
    After long years,
How should I greet thee?
    With silence and tears.

98

I Find No Peace

[handwritten: → in death too]

[handwritten: Henry the 8th → Era, Love ↑ 16th century]

SIR THOMAS WYATT

[handwritten left margin: Emasculated, Juvenile. No control]

[handwritten: Figurative death]

[handwritten: entitled] *[handwritten: → if war context, disillusionment, PTSD?]*

I find no peace, and all my war is done. *[handwritten: "And" continued conflict, Pendulous]*
I fear and hope. I burn and freeze like ice.
I fly above the wind, yet can I not arise; *[handwritten: Same feeling, they live in one another]*
And nought I have, and all the world I season. *[handwritten: Material]*
That loseth nor locketh holdeth me in prison
And holdeth me not—yet can I scape no wise— *[handwritten: imprisoning dashes]*
Nor letteth me live nor die at my device, *[handwritten: agency]*
And yet of death it giveth me occasion. *[handwritten: Juvenile]* *[handwritten: → poem to appeal to her]*
Without eyen I see, and without tongue I plain. *[handwritten: Melodramatic]*
I desire to perish, and yet I ask health. *[handwritten: Masochistic?]*
I love another, and thus I hate myself. *[handwritten left: not him? ← Another ↓ lover?]*
I feed me in sorrow and laugh in all my pain; *[handwritten: Madness]*
Likewise displeaseth me both life and death, *[handwritten: Purgatorial]*
And my delight is causer of this strife.

[handwritten: → love, fleeting bitter happinesses]

[handwritten: Self esteem, Post-rejection]

[handwritten: Emotional poles/superlatives + random paradoxes]

[handwritten: Instilled Passivity]

season] relish
That loseth nor locketh holdeth me in prison] that which (i.e. love) neither loosens the bonds that
    tie me, nor fully constrains me, still imprisons me
scape no wise] escape by any means
at my device] by my own will or power
eyen] eyes
plain] complain
feed me in] am revived by

99

I Hear an Army…

JAMES JOYCE

I hear an army charging upon the land,
   And the thunder of horses plunging, foam about their knees;
Arrogant, in black armour, behind them stand,
   Disdaining the reins, with fluttering whips, the charioteers.

They cry unto the night their battle-name:
   I moan in sleep when I hear afar their whirling laughter.
They cleave the gloom of dreams, a blinding flame,
   Clanging, clanging upon the heart as upon an anvil.

They come shaking in triumph their long, green hair:
   They come out of the sea and run shouting by the shore.
My heart, have you no wisdom thus to despair?
   My love, my love, my love, why have you left me alone?

100

Love Arm'd

APHRA BEHN

Love in Fantastique Triumph satt,
Whilst Bleeding Hearts a round him flow'd,
For whom Fresh paines he did Create,
And strange Tyranick power he show'd;
From thy Bright Eyes he took his fire,
Which round about, in sport he hurl'd;
But 'twas from mine, he took desire,
Enough to undo the Amorous World.

From me he took his sighs and tears,
From thee his Pride and Crueltie;
From me his Languishments and Feares,
And every Killing Dart from thee;
Thus thou and I, the God have arm'd,
And sett him up a Deity;
But my poor Heart alone is harm'd,
Whilst thine the Victor is, and free.

101

Amoretti, Sonnet 86

EDMUND SPENSER

Since I did leave the presence of my love,
Many long weary days I have outworn,
And many nights, that slowly seem'd to move
Their sad protract from evening until morn.
For, whenas day the heaven doth adorn,
I wish that night the noyous day would end:
And, whenas night hath us of light forlorn,
I wish that day would shortly reascend.
Thus I the time with expectation spend,
And feign my grief with changes to beguile,
That further seems his term still to extend,
And maketh every minute seem a mile.
        So sorrow still doth seem too long to last;
        But joyous hours do fly away too fast.

protract] extended progress
whenas] while, at the moment when
noyous] troubling, distressing

102

Rooms

CHARLOTTE MEW

I remember rooms that have had their part
In the steady slowing down of the heart.
The room in Paris, the room at Geneva,
The little damp room with the seaweed smell,
And that ceaseless maddening sound of the tide—
    Rooms where for good or for ill—things died.
But there is the room where we (two) lie dead,
Though every morning we seem to wake and might just as well seem
    to sleep again
    As we shall somewhere in the other quieter, dustier bed
    Out there in the sun—in the rain.

103

Love in a Life

ROBERT BROWNING

I

Room after room,
I hunt the house through
We inhabit together.
Heart, fear nothing, for, heart, thou shalt find her—
Next time, herself!—not the trouble behind her
Left in the curtain, the couch's perfume!
As she brushed it, the cornice-wreath blossomed anew:
Yon looking-glass gleamed at the wave of her feather.

II

Yet the day wears,
And door succeeds door;
I try the fresh fortune—
Range the wide house from the wing to the centre.
Still the same chance! she goes out as I enter.
Spend my whole day in the quest,—who cares?
But 't is twilight, you see,—with such suites to explore,
Such closets to search, such alcoves to importune!

cornice-wreath] ceiling decoration

104

Homecoming

LENRIE PETERS

The present reigned supreme
  Like the shallow floods over the gutters
Over the raw paths where we had been,
  The house with the shutters.

Too strange the sudden change
  Of the times we buried when we left
The time before we had properly arranged
  The memories that we kept.

Our sapless roots have fed
  The wind-swept seedlings of another age.
Luxuriant weeds have grown where we led
  The Virgins to the water's edge.

There at the edge of the town
  Just by the burial ground
Stands the house without a shadow
  Lived in by new skeletons.

That is all that is left
  To greet us on the home-coming
After we have paced the world
  And longed for returning.

105

I Years had been from Home

EMILY DICKINSON

I Years had been from Home
And now before the Door
I dared not enter, lest a Face
I never saw before

Stare stolid into mine
And ask my Business there –
"My Business but a Life I left
Was such remaining there?"

I leaned upon the Awe –
I lingered with Before –
The Second like an Ocean rolled
And broke against my ear –

I laughed a crumbling Laugh
That I could fear a Door
Who Consternation compassed
And never winced before.

I fitted to the Latch
My Hand, with trembling care
Lest back the awful Door should spring
And leave me in the Floor –

Then moved my Fingers off
As cautiously as Glass
And held my ears, and like a Thief
Fled gasping from the House –

106

Waterfall

LAURIS EDMOND

I do not ask for youth, nor for delay
in the rising of time's irreversible river
that takes the jewelled arc of the waterfall
in which I glimpse, minute by glinting minute,
all that I have and all I am always losing
as sunlight lights each drop fast, fast falling.

I do not dream that you, young again,
might come to me darkly in love's green darkness
where the dust of the bracken spices the air
moss, crushed, gives out an astringent sweetness
and water holds our reflections
motionless, as if for ever.

It is enough now to come into a room
and find the kindness we have for each other
– calling it love – in eyes that are shrewd
but trustful still, face chastened by years
of careful judgement; to sit in the afternoons
in mild conversation, without nostalgia.

But when you leave me, with your jauntiness
sinewed by resolution more than strength
– suddenly then I love you with a quick
intensity, remembering that water,
however luminous and grand, falls fast
and only once to the dark pool below.

107

When You are Old

WILLIAM BUTLER YEATS

When you are old and grey and full of sleep,
  And nodding by the fire, take down this book,
  And slowly read, and dream of the soft look
Your eyes had once, and of their shadows deep;

How many loved your moments of glad grace,
  And loved your beauty with love false or true;
  But one man loved the pilgrim soul in you,
And loved the sorrows of your changing face;

And bending down beside the glowing bars,
  Murmur, a little sadly, how Love fled
  And paced upon the mountains overhead,
And hid his face amid a crowd of stars.

glowing bars] the grate of the fire-hearth

108

Verses Written on Her Death-bed at Bath to Her Husband in London

MARY MONCK ('MARINDA')

Thou who dost all my worldly thoughts employ,
Thou pleasing source of all my earthly joy,
Thou tenderest husband and thou dearest friend,
To thee this first, this last adieu I send.
At length the conqueror Death asserts his right,
And will for ever veil me from thy sight.
He woos me to him with a cheerful grace,
And not one terror clouds his meagre face.
He promises a lasting rest from pain,
And shows that all life's fleeting joys are vain.
The eternal scenes of Heaven he sets in view,
And tells me that no other joys are true,
But love, fond love, would yet resist his power,
Would fain awhile defer the parting hour.
He brings thy mourning image to my eyes,
And would obstruct my journey to the skies.
But say, thou dearest, thou unwearied friend,
Say, shouldst thou grieve to see my sorrows end?
Thou knowest a painful pilgrimage I've passed,
And shouldst thou grieve that rest is come at last?
Rather rejoice to see me shake off life,
And die, as I have lived, thy faithful wife.

pilgrimage] spiritual journey

109

The Exequy

HENRY KING

Accept, thou shrine of my dead Saint!
Instead of dirges this complaint;
And for sweet flowers to crown thy hearse,
Receive a strew of weeping verse
From thy griev'd friend, whom thou might'st see
Quite melted into tears for thee.
　Dear loss! since thy untimely fate
My task hath been to meditate
On thee, on thee: thou art the book,
The library whereon I look
Though almost blind. For thee (lov'd clay!)
I languish out, not live the day,
Using no other exercise
But what I practise with mine eyes.
By which wet glasses I find out
How lazily time creeps about
To one that mourns: this, only this
My exercise and bus'ness is:
So I compute the weary hours
With sighs dissolved into showers.
　Nor wonder if my time go thus
Backward and most preposterous;
Thou hast benighted me. Thy set
This eve of blackness did beget,
Who wast my day, (though overcast
Before thou had'st thy noon-tide passed)
And I remember must in tears,
Thou scarce had'st seen so many years

Exequy] funeral ceremony

As day tells hours. By thy clear sun
My love and fortune first did run;
But thou wilt never more appear
Folded within my hemisphere:
Since both thy light and motion
Like a fled star is fall'n and gone;
And twixt me and my soul's dear wish
The earth now interposed is,
With such a strange eclipse doth make
As ne'er was read in almanake.
　　I could allow thee for a time
To darken me and my sad clime,
Were it a month, a year, or ten,
I would thy exile live till then;
And all that space my mirth adjourn
So thou wouldst promise to return;
And putting off thy ashy shroud
At length disperse this sorrow's cloud.
　　But woe is me! the longest date
Too narrow is to calculate
These empty hopes. Never shall I
Be so much blest, as to descry
A glimpse of thee, till that day come
Which shall the earth to cinders doom,
And a fierce fever must calcine
The body of this world, like thine
(My Little World!). That fit of fire
Once off, our bodies shall aspire
To our souls' bliss: then we shall rise,
And view ourselves with clearer eyes
In that calm region, where no night
Can hide us from each other's sight.

Folded . . . hemisphere] contained . . . part of the globe
almanake] i.e. almanac; astronomical calendar
longest . . . Too narrow is . . . calculate] most distant . . . is too small . . . determine by arithmetic
descry] discern
that day] i.e. the Apocalypse, the Day of Judgement
to cinders doom] sentence to fiery destruction
calcine] reduce to ashes, consume with fire
fit] temporary explosion
Once off] i.e. once over

Meantime, thou hast her, earth: much good
May my harm do thee. Since it stood
With Heaven's will I might not call
Her longer mine, I give thee all
My short-liv'd right and interest
In her, whom living I lov'd best:
With a most free and bounteous grief,
I give thee what I could not keep.
Be kind to her, and prithee look
Thou write into thy Doomsday book
Each parcel of this rarity
Which in thy casket shrin'd doth lie:
See that thou make thy reck'ning straight,
And yield her back again by weight;
For thou must audit on thy trust
Each grain and atom of this dust:
As thou wilt answer Him, that lent,
Not gave thee, my dear monument.
    So close the ground, and 'bout her shade
Black curtains draw, my bride is laid.
    Sleep on (my love!) in thy cold bed
Never to be disquieted,
My last good night! Thou wilt not wake
Till I thy fate shall overtake:
Till age, or grief, or sickness must
Marry my body to that dust
It so much loves; and fill the room
My heart keeps empty in thy tomb.
Stay for me there; I will not fail
To meet thee in that hollow vale.
And think not much of my delay;
I am already on the way,
And follow thee with all the speed
Desire can make, or sorrows breed.

Doomsday book] universal register of our faults and virtues
make thy reck'ning straight] make an exact calculation

Each minute is a short degree
And ev'ry hour a step towards thee.
At night when I betake to rest,
Next morn I rise nearer my west
Of life, almost by eight hours' sail,
Than when sleep breath'd his drowsy gale.
    Thus from the sun my bottom steers,
And my days' compass downward bears.
Nor labour I to stem the tide,
Through which to thee I swiftly glide.
    'Tis true; with shame and grief I yield,
Thou, like the van, first took'st the field,
And gotten hast the victory
In thus adventuring to die
Before me; whose more years might crave
A just precedence in the grave.
But hark! My pulse, like a soft drum
Beats my approach, tells thee I come;
And slow howe'er my marches be,
I shall at last sit down by thee.
    The thought of this bids me go on,
And wait my dissolution
With hope and comfort. Dear! (forgive
The crime) I am content to live
Divided, with but half a heart,
Till we shall meet and never part.

van] the foremost part of an army

110

Growing Old

MATTHEW ARNOLD

What is it to grow old?
Is it to lose the glory of the form,
The lustre of the eye?
Is it for beauty to forego her wreath?
–Yes, but not this alone.

Is it to feel our strength–
Not our bloom only, but our strength–decay?
Is it to feel each limb
Grow stiffer, every function less exact,
Each nerve more loosely strung?

Yes, this, and more; but not
Ah, 'tis not what in youth we dreamed 'twould be!
'Tis not to have our life
Mellowed and softened as with sunset glow,
A golden day's decline.

'Tis not to see the world
As from a height, with rapt prophetic eyes,
And heart profoundly stirred;
And weep, and feel the fullness of the past,
The years that are no more.

It is to spend long days
And not once feel that we were ever young;
It is to add, immured
In the hot prison of the present, month
To month with weary pain.

It is to suffer this,
And feel but half, and feebly, what we feel.
Deep in our hidden heart
Festers the dull remembrance of a change,
But no emotion–none.

It is–last stage of all–
When we are frozen up within, and quite
The phantom of ourselves,
To hear the world applaud the hollow ghost
Which blamed the living man.

last stage of all] an echo of 'Last scene of all', from the 'Seven Ages of Man' speech in Shakespeare's
  As You Like It

111

Old Man

JAMES HENRY

At six years old I had before mine eyes
A picture painted, like the rainbow, bright,
But far, far off in th' unapproachable distance.
With all my childish heart I longed to reach it,
And strove and strove the livelong day in vain,
Advancing with slow step some few short yards
But not perceptibly the distance lessening.
At threescore years old, when almost within
Grasp of my outstretched arms the selfsame picture
With all its beauteous colors painted bright,
I'm backward from it further borne each day
By an invisible, compulsive force,
Gradual but yet so steady, sure, and rapid,
That at threescore and ten I'll from the picture
Be even more distant than I was at six.

Very Old Man

JAMES HENRY

I well remember how some threescore years
And ten ago, a helpless babe, I toddled
From chair to chair about my mother's chamber,
Feeling, as 'twere, my way in the new world
And foolishly afraid of, or, as 't might be,
Foolishly pleased with, th' unknown objects round me.
And now with stiffened joints I sit all day
In one of those same chairs, as foolishly
Hoping or fearing something from me hid
Behind the thick, dark veil which I see hourly
And minutely on every side round closing
And from my view all objects shutting out.

112

Rhyme of the Dead Self

A.R.D. FAIRBURN

Tonight I have taken all that I was
and strangled him that pale lily-white lad
I have choked him with these my hands these claws
catching him as he lay a-dreaming in his bed.

Then chuckling I dragged out his foolish brains
that were full of pretty love-tales heighho the holly
and emptied them holus bolus to the drains
those dreams of love oh what ruinous folly.

He is dead pale youth and he shall not rise
on the third day or any other day
sloughed like a snakeskin there he lies
and he shall not trouble me again for aye.

heighho the holly] a reference to the chorus of the song 'Blow, blow, thou winter wind' in Shakespeare's
  As You Like It (2.7)
holus bolus] wholesale, in one go

113

Stanzas Written in Dejection, Near Naples

PERCY BYSSHE SHELLEY

I

The sun is warm, the sky is clear,
   The waves are dancing fast and bright,
Blue isles and snowy mountains wear
   The purple noon's transparent might,
   The breath of the moist earth is light,
Around its unexpanded buds;
   Like many a voice of one delight,
The winds, the birds, the ocean floods,
The City's voice itself, is soft like Solitude's.

II

I see the Deep's untrampled floor
   With green and purple seaweeds strown;
I see the waves upon the shore,
   Like light dissolved in star-showers, thrown:
   I sit upon the sands alone,—
The lightning of the noontide ocean
   Is flashing round me, and a tone
Arises from its measured motion,
How sweet! did any heart now share in my emotion.

III

Alas! I have nor hope nor health,
    Nor peace within nor calm around,
Nor that content surpassing wealth
    The sage in meditation found,
    And walked with inward glory crowned—
Nor fame, nor power, nor love, nor leisure.
    Others I see whom these surround—
Smiling they live, and call life pleasure;—
To me that cup has been dealt in another measure.

IV

Yet now despair itself is mild,
    Even as the winds and waters are;
I could lie down like a tired child,
    And weep away the life of care
    Which I have borne and yet must bear,
Till death like sleep might steal on me,
    And I might feel in the warm air
My cheek grow cold, and hear the sea
Breathe o'er my dying brain its last monotony.

V

Some might lament that I were cold,
    As I, when this sweet day is gone,
Which my lost heart, too soon grown old,
    Insults with this untimely moan;
    They might lament—for I am one
Whom men love not,—and yet regret,
    Unlike this day, which, when the sun
Shall on its stainless glory set,
Will linger, though enjoyed, like joy in memory yet.

114

On This Day I Complete My Thirty-Sixth Year

GEORGE GORDON, LORD BYRON

Messalonghi. January 22nd, 1824.

'Tis time this heart should be unmoved,
   Since others it hath ceased to move:
Yet though I cannot be beloved,
          Still let me love!

My days are in the yellow leaf;
   The flowers and fruits of Love are gone;
The worm—the canker, and the grief
          Are mine alone!

The fire that on my bosom preys
   Is lone as some Volcanic Isle;
No torch is kindled at its blaze
          A funeral pile!

The hope, the fear, the jealous care,
   The exalted portion of the pain
And power of Love I cannot share,
          But wear the chain.

But 'tis not *thus*—and 'tis not *here*
   Such thoughts should shake my Soul, nor *now*
Where Glory decks the hero's bier
          Or binds his brow.

Messalonghi] a Greek coastal city, besieged during Greece's war of independence, during which
   Byron died (on 19 April 1824)
in the yellow leaf] an echo of Shakespeare's *Macbeth* (5.3): 'my way of life | Is fall'n into the
   sear, the yellow leaf'

The Sword, the Banner, and the Field,
  Glory and Greece around us see!
The Spartan borne upon his shield
               Was not more free!

Awake (not Greece—she *is* awake!)
  Awake, my Spirit! think through *whom*
Thy life-blood tracks its parent lake
               And then strike home!

Tread those reviving passions down
  Unworthy Manhood—unto thee
Indifferent should the smile or frown
               Of Beauty be.

If thou regret'st thy Youth, *why live*?
  The land of honourable Death
Is here:—up to the Field, and give
               Away thy Breath!

Seek out—less often sought than found—
  A Soldier's Grave, for thee the best;
Then look around, and choose thy Ground,
               And take thy Rest!

the Field] i.e. the battlefield
Spartan borne upon his shield] i.e. the fallen hero of Greece's ancient enemy, carried back from
  the battlefield on his own shield

115

Nearing Forty

DEREK WALCOTT

(for John Figueroa)

*The irregular combination of fanciful invention may
delight awhile by that novelty of which the common
satiety of life sends us all in quest. But the pleasures of
sudden wonder are soon exhausted and the mind can
only repose on the stability of truth . . .*
                                        SAMUEL JOHNSON

Insomniac since four, hearing this narrow,
rigidly-metred, early-rising rain
recounting, as its coolness numbs the marrow,
that I am nearing forty, nearer the weak
vision thickening to a frosted pane,
nearer the day when I may judge my work
by the bleak modesty of middle-age
as a false dawn, fireless and average,
which would be just, because your life bled for
the household truth, the style past metaphor
that finds its parallel however wretched
in simple, shining lines, in pages stretched
plain as a bleaching bedsheet under a guttering rainspout, glad for the sputter
of occasional insight; you who foresaw

John Figueroa] (1920–1999), Jamaican poet and teacher
Samuel Johnson] (1709–1784), English scholar and poet

ambition as a searing meteor
will fumble a damp match, and smiling, settle
for the dry wheezing of a dented kettle,
for vision narrower than a louvre's gap,
then watching your leaves thin, recall how deep
prodigious cynicism plants its seed,
gauges our seasons by this year's end rain
which, as greenhorns at school, we'd
call conventional for convectional;
or you will rise and set your lines to work
with sadder joy but steadier elation,
until the night when you can really sleep,
measuring how imagination
ebbs, conventional as any water-clerk
who weighs the force of lightly-falling rain,
which, as the new moon moves it, does its work,
even when it seems to weep.

116

Late Wisdom

GEORGE CRABBE

We've trod the maze of error round,
  Long wandering in the winding glade;
And now the torch of truth is found,
  It only shows us where we strayed:
By long experience taught, we know—
  Can rightly judge of friends and foes;
Can all the worth of these allow,
  And all the faults discern in those.

Now, 'tis our boast that we can quell
  The wildest passions in their rage,
Can their destructive force repel,
  And their impetuous wrath assuage.—
Ah, Virtue! dost thou arm when now
  This bold rebellious race are fled?
When all these tyrants rest, and thou
  Art warring with the mighty dead?

117

Now Let No Charitable Hope

ELINOR MORTON WYLIE

Now let no charitable hope
Confuse my mind with images
Of eagle and of antelope:
I am by nature none of these.

I was, being human, born alone;
I am, being woman, hard beset;
I live by squeezing from a stone
What little nourishment I get.

In masks outrageous and austere
The years go by in single file;
But none has merited my fear,
And none has quite escaped my smile.

118

from *The Vanity of Human Wishes*

SAMUEL JOHNSON

The Tenth Satire of Juvenal, Imitated

Let observation with extensive view,
Survey mankind, from China to Peru;
Remark each anxious toil, each eager strife,
And watch the busy scenes of crowded life;
Then say how hope and fear, desire and hate,
O'erspread with snares the clouded maze of fate,
Where wav'ring man, betray'd by vent'rous pride
To tread the dreary paths without a guide,
As treach'rous phantoms in the mist delude,
Shuns fancied ills, or chases airy good.
How rarely reason guides the stubborn choice,
Rules the bold hand, or prompts the suppliant voice,
How nations sink, by darling schemes oppress'd,
When vengeance listens to the fool's request.
Fate wings with ev'ry wish th' afflictive dart,
Each gift of nature, and each grace of art,
With fatal heat impetuous courage glows,
With fatal sweetness elocution flows,
Impeachment stops the speaker's pow'rful breath,
And restless fire precipitates on death.

But scarce observ'd the knowing and the bold,
Fall in the gen'ral massacre of gold;
Wide-wasting pest! that rages unconfin'd,
And crowds with crimes the records of mankind,
For gold his sword the hireling ruffian draws,
For gold the hireling judge distorts the laws;
Wealth heap'd on wealth, nor truth nor safety buys,
The dangers gather as the treasures rise.

Juvenal] an Ancient Roman satirical poet (active *c*. 100 AD)   wings] furnishes
vent'rous] (venturous), ambitious, enterprising   Impeachment] hindrance, legal prosecution

119

from *An Essay on Criticism*

ALEXANDER POPE

A little learning is a dangerous thing;
Drink deep, or taste not the Pierian spring:
There shallow draughts intoxicate the brain,
And drinking largely sobers us again.
Fired at first sight with what the Muse imparts,
In fearless youth we tempt the heights of Arts;
While from the bounded level of our mind
Short views we take, nor see the lengths behind,
But, more advanced, behold with strange surprise
New distant scenes of endless science rise!
So pleased at first the towering Alps we try,
Mount o'er the vales, and seem to tread the sky;
The eternal snows appear already past,
And the first clouds and mountains seem the last:
But those attained, we tremble to survey
The growing labours of the lengthened way;
The increasing prospect tires our wandering eyes,
Hills peep o'er hills, and Alps on Alps arise!

Pierian spring] the fount of poetry and learning on Mount Olympus, the home of the Muses in
   classical mythology
Muse] one of the Nine personifications of the arts and sciences in classical mythology

120

The Character of a Happy Life

HENRY WOTTON

How happy is he born and taught
That serveth not another's will;
Whose armour is his honest thought,
And simple truth his utmost skill!

Whose passions not his masters are;
Whose soul is still prepared for death,
Untied unto the world by care
Of public fame or private breath;

Who envies none that chance doth raise,
Nor vice; who never understood
How deepest wounds are given by praise;
Nor rules of state, but rules of good;

Who hath his life from rumours freed;
Whose conscience is his strong retreat;
Whose state can neither flatterers feed,
Nor ruin make oppressors great;

Who God doth late and early pray
More of His grace than gifts to lend;
And entertains the harmless day
With a religious book or friend;

——This man is freed from servile bands
Of hope to rise or fear to fall:
Lord of himself, though not of lands,
And having nothing, yet hath all.

Part 5

War, Sleep, and Death

121

Distant Fields / ANZAC Parade

RHIAN GALLAGHER

Medalled, ribboned chests, an effort
carried through them, the war
still going on inside their heads,
gathered up for roll call.

Where all the flowers had gone
came a quiet of ash,
line after line after line.

As if the grainy footage played above the leafy street
my father lifted me on to his shoulders to see.

My uncles looked to the back of the one in front,
marching to the heart-beat drum.

At end of Mass the bugle rose,
life unto life, a single breath
took flight into the bird-light zone.

ANZAC] (*acronym*) the Australian and New Zealand Army Corps

122

Lament for the Country Soldiers

LES MURRAY

The king of honour, louder than of England
Cried on the young men to a gallant day
And ate the hearts of those who would not go

For the gathering ranks were the Chosen Company
That each man in his lifetime seeks, and finds,
Some for an hour, some beyond recall.

When to prove their life, they set their lives at risk
And in the ruins of horizons died
One out of four, in the spreading rose of their honour

They didn't see the badge upon their hat
Was the ancient sword that points in all directions.
The symbol hacked the homesteads even so.

The static farms withstood it to the end,
The galloping telegrams ceasing, the exchanges
Ringing no more in the night of the stunned violin,

And in the morning of insult, the equal remember
Ribaldry, madness, the wire jerking with friends,
Ironic salutes for the claimants of the fox-hunt

As, camped under tin like rabbiters in death's gully
They stemmed the endless weather of grey men and steel
And, first of all armies, stormed into great fields.

exchanges] i.e. telephone exchanges: the offices that mediated telephone and telegram traffic
claimants of the fox-hunt] i.e. those of the officer-class whose social engagements included fox-hunting

But it was a weight beyond speech, the proven nation
On beasts and boys. Newborn experiment withered.
Dull horror rotting miles wide in the memory of green.

Touching money, the white feather crumpled to ash,
Cold lies grew quickly in the rank decades
As, far away, the ascendant conquered courage,

And we debauched the faith we were to keep
With the childless singing on the morning track,
The Sportsmen's Thousand leaping on the mountains,

Now growing remote, beneath their crumbling farms,
In the district light, their fading companies
With the king of honour, deeper than of England

Though the stones of increase glitter with their names.

The Sportsmen's Thousand] a phrase from the ANZAC recruiting posters

123

"I Have a Rendezvous with Death"

ALAN SEEGER

I have a rendezvous with Death
At some disputed barricade,
When Spring comes back with rustling shade
And apple-blossoms fill the air—
I have a rendezvous with Death
When Spring brings back blue days and fair.

It may be he shall take my hand
And lead me into his dark land
And close my eyes and quench my breath—
It may be I shall pass him still.
I have a rendezvous with Death
On some scarred slope of battered hill,
When Spring comes round again this year
And the first meadow-flowers appear.

God knows 'twere better to be deep
Pillowed in silk and scented down,
Where love throbs out in blissful sleep,
Pulse nigh to pulse, and breath to breath,
Where hushed awakenings are dear…
But I've a rendezvous with Death
At midnight in some flaming town,
When Spring trips north again this year,
And I to my pledged word am true,
I shall not fail that rendezvous.

124

The Death-Bed

SIEGFRIED SASSOON

He drowsed and was aware of silence heaped
Round him, unshaken as the steadfast walls;
Aqueous like floating rays of amber light,
Soaring and quivering in the wings of sleep.
Silence and safety; and his mortal shore
Lipped by the inward, moonless waves of death.

Someone was holding water to his mouth.
He swallowed, unresisting; moaned and dropped
Through crimson gloom to darkness; and forgot
The opiate throb and ache that was his wound.
Water – calm, sliding green above the weir.
Water – a sky-lit alley for his boat,
Bird-voiced, and bordered with reflected flowers
And shaken hues of summer; drifting down,
He dipped contented oars, and sighed, and slept.

Night, with a gust of wind, was in the ward,
Blowing the curtain to a glimmering curve.
Night. He was blind; he could not see the stars
Glinting among the wraiths of wandering cloud;
Queer blots of colour, purple, scarlet, green,
Flickered and faded in his drowning eyes.

Aqueous] watery

Rain – he could hear it rustling through the dark;
Fragrance and passionless music woven as one;
Warm rain on drooping roses; pattering showers
That soak the woods; not the harsh rain that sweeps
Behind the thunder, but a trickling peace,
Gently and slowly washing life away.

He stirred, shifting his body; then the pain
Leapt like a prowling beast, and gripped and tore
His groping dreams with grinding claws and fangs.
But someone was beside him; soon he lay
Shuddering because that evil thing had passed.
And death, who'd stepped toward him, paused and stared.

Light many lamps and gather round his bed.
Lend him your eyes, warm blood, and will to live.
Speak to him; rouse him; you may save him yet.
He's young; he hated War; how should he die
When cruel old campaigners win safe through?

But death replied: 'I choose him.' So he went,
And there was silence in the summer night;
Silence and safety; and the veils of sleep.
Then, far away, the thudding of the guns.

125

A Wife in London (December, 1899)

THOMAS HARDY

I--The Tragedy
She sits in the tawny vapour
  That the City lanes have uprolled,
  Behind whose webby fold on fold
Like a waning taper
  The street-lamp glimmers cold.

A messenger's knock cracks smartly,
  Flashed news is in her hand
  Of meaning it dazes to understand
Though shaped so shortly:
  He--has fallen--in the far South Land . . .

II--The Irony
'Tis the morrow; the fog hangs thicker,
  The postman nears and goes:
  A letter is brought whose lines disclose
By the firelight flicker
  His hand, whom the worm now knows:

Fresh--firm--penned in highest feather –
  Page-full of his hoped return,
  And of home-planned jaunts by brake and burn
In the summer weather,
  And of new love that they would learn.

waning taper] guttering candle
Flashed] conveyed by electricity
South Land] i.e. South Africa (the site of the second Boer War, 1899–1902)
in highest feather] in high spirits

126

Song

(On seeing dead bodies floating off the Cape)

ALUN LEWIS

The first month of his absence
I was numb and sick
And where he'd left his promise
Life did not turn or kick.
The seed, the seed of love was sick.

The second month my eyes were sunk
In the darkness of despair,
And my bed was like a grave
And his ghost was lying there.
And my heart was sick with care.

The third month of his going
I thought I heard him say
'Our course deflected slightly
On the thirty-second day—'
The tempest blew his words away.

And he was lost among the waves,
His ship rolled helpless in the sea,
The fourth month of his voyage
He shouted grievously
'Beloved, do not think of me.'

the Cape] i.e. the Cape of Good Hope, South Africa; the poet was aboard a British troopship en route to
India when diverted to attend the aftermath of a submarine attack on another ship

The flying fish like kingfishers
Skim the sea's bewildered crests, *Tranquil, life goes on, specific descriptions of this ocean*
The whales blow steaming fountains,
The seagulls have no nests *Time no longer counted,*
Where my lover sways and rests. *Poignant   measured, becomes this endless*

We never thought to buy and sell
Resignation This life that blooms or withers in the leaf, *Naïve*
& understanding And I'll not stir, so he sleeps well,
Though cell by cell the coral reef *gentle gradual atomisation into massive sea*
then Builds an eternity of grief.

But oh! the drag and dullness of my Self;
The turning seasons wither in my head; *forgetting, decaying*
All this slowness, all this hardness, *flow time, the pain*
The nearness that is waiting in my bed, *ghost*
The gradual self-effacement of the dead.

Gotta die to be with him

127

from *Blenheim*

JOHN PHILIPS

                                        Now from each van
The brazen instruments of death discharge
Horrible flames, and turbid streaming clouds
Of smoke sulphureous; intermixed with these
Large globous irons fly, of dreadful hiss,
Singeing the air, and from long distance bring
Surprising slaughter; on each side they fly
By chains connexed, and with destructive sweep
Behead whole troops at once; the hairy scalps
Are whirled aloof, while numerous trunks bestrow
Th' ensanguined field; with latent mischief stored
Show'rs of grenadoes rain, by sudden burst
Disploding murd'rous bowels, fragments of steel,
And stones, and glass, and nitrous grain adust.
A thousand ways at once the shivered orbs
Fly diverse, working torment and foul rout
With deadly bruise, and gashes furrowed deep.
Of pain impatient, the high-prancing steeds
Disdain the curb, and, flinging to and fro,
Spurn their dismounted riders; they expire
Indignant, by unhostile wounds destroyed.

Blenheim] the Battle won in Germany in 1704 by the English Duke of Marlborough, commanding
    a coalition army against the French
van] foremost military unit, vanguard
By chains connexed] i.e. chain-shot (by which two spherical or hemi-spherical cannon balls were
    connected by a chain to increase their murderous range and power)
whole troops] i.e. entire ranks of soldiers
ensanguined] bloodied
grenadoes] grenades
bowels] i.e. contents

Thus through each army death in various shapes
Prevailed; here mangled limbs, here brains and gore
Lie clotted; lifeless some: with anguish these
Gnashing, and loud laments invoking aid,
Unpitied and unheard; the louder din
Of guns, and trumpets' clang, and solemn sound
Of drums, o'ercame their groans.

128

After Blenheim

ROBERT SOUTHEY

It was a summer evening,
   Old Kaspar's work was done,
And he before his cottage door
   Was sitting in the sun;
And by him sported on the green
His little grandchild Wilhelmine.

She saw her brother Peterkin
   Roll something large and round
Which he beside the rivulet
   In playing there had found;
He came to ask what he had found
That was so large and smooth and round.

Old Kaspar took it from the boy
   Who stood expectant by;
And then the old man shook his head,
   And with a natural sigh
''Tis some poor fellow's skull,' said he,
'Who fell in the great victory.'

'I find them in the garden,
   For there's many here about;
And often when I go to plough
   The ploughshare turns them out.
For many thousand men,' said he,
'Were slain in that great victory.'

Blenheim] the Battle won in Germany in 1704 by the English Duke of Marlborough, commanding
   a coalition army against the French
Kaspar . . . Wilhelmine . . . Peterkin] i.e. German names

'Now tell us what 'twas all about,'
　　Young Peterkin he cries;
And little Wilhelmine looks up
　　With wonder-waiting eyes;
'Now tell us all about the war,
And what they fought each other for.'

'It was the English,' Kaspar cried,
　　'Who put the French to rout;
But what they fought each other for
　　I could not well make out.
But everybody said,' quoth he,
'That 'twas a famous victory.

'My father lived at Blenheim then,
　　Yon little stream hard by;
They burnt his dwelling to the ground,
　　And he was forced to fly:
So with his wife and child he fled,
Nor had he where to rest his head.

'With fire and sword the country round
　　Was wasted far and wide,
And many a childing mother then
　　And newborn baby died:
But things like that, you know, must be
At every famous victory.

'They say it was a shocking sight
　　After the field was won;
For many thousand bodies here
　　Lay rotting in the sun:
But things like that, you know, must be
After a famous victory.

childing] pregnant

'Great praise the Duke of Marlbro' won
   And our good Prince Eugene;'
'Why, 'twas a very wicked thing!'
   Said little Wilhelmine;
'Nay . . nay . . my little girl,' quoth he,
'It was a famous victory.

'And everybody praised the Duke
   Who this great fight did win.'
'But what good came of it at last?'
   Quoth little Peterkin:—
'Why that I cannot tell,' said he,
'But 'twas a famous victory.'

Duke of Marlbro' . . . Prince Eugene] the English Duke of Marlborough and the Franco-Austrian
   Prince Eugen of Savoy, the principal commanders of the Allied army

129

from *Fears in Solitude*

SAMUEL TAYLOR COLERIDGE

                              Thankless too for peace,
(Peace long preserved by fleets and perilous seas)
Secure from actual warfare, we have loved
To swell the war-whoop, passionate for war!
Alas! for ages ignorant of all
Its ghastlier workings, (famine or blue plague,
Battle, or siege, or flight through wintry snows,)
We, this whole people, have been clamorous
For war and bloodshed; animating sports,
The which we pay for as a thing to talk of,
Spectators and not combatants! No guess
Anticipative of a wrong unfelt,
No speculation on contingency,
However dim and vague, too vague and dim
To yield a justifying cause; and forth,
(Stuffed out with big preamble, holy names,
And adjurations of the God in Heaven,)
We send our mandates for the certain death
Of thousands and ten thousands! Boys and girls,
And women, that would groan to see a child
Pull off an insect's leg, all read of war,
The best amusement for our morning meal!
The poor wretch, who has learnt his only prayers
From curses, who knows scarcely words enough
To ask a blessing from his Heavenly Father,

speculation on contingency] consideration of uncertainty
justifying cause] justification for war, *casus belli*

Becomes a fluent phraseman, absolute
And technical in victories and defeats,
And all our dainty terms for fratricide;
Terms which we trundle smoothly o'er our tongues
Like mere abstractions, empty sounds to which
We join no feeling and attach no form!
As if the soldier died without a wound;
As if the fibres of this godlike frame
Were gored without a pang; as if the wretch,
Who fell in battle, doing bloody deeds,
Passed off to Heaven, translated and not killed;
As though he had no wife to pine for him,
No God to judge him! Therefore, evil days
Are coming on us, O my countrymen!
And what if all-avenging Providence,
Strong and retributive, should make us know
The meaning of our words, force us to feel
The desolation and the agony
Of our fierce doings?

130

Soldier, Rest!

Things heard by soldier

SIR WALTER SCOTT

Soldier, rest! thy warfare o'er,
  Sleep the sleep that knows not breaking;
Dream of battled fields no more,
  Days of danger, nights of waking.
In our isle's enchanted hall,
  Hands unseen thy couch are strewing,
Fairy strains of music fall,
  Every sense in slumber dewing.
Soldier, rest! thy warfare o'er,
Dream of fighting fields no more:
Sleep the sleep that knows not breaking,
Morn of toil, nor night of waking.

Peaceful, mystic

Hypnotic, lulling

No rude sound shall reach thine ear,
  Armour's clang, or war-steed champing,
Trump nor pibroch summon here
  Mustering clan, or squadron tramping.
Yet the lark's shrill fife may come
  At the day-break from the fallow,
And the bittern sound his drum,
  Booming from the sedgy shallow.
Ruder sounds shall none be near,
Guards nor warders challenge here,
Here's no war-steed's neigh and champing,
Shouting clans, or squadrons stamping.

Aural, Plosive

Shan't wake him, *Blend of Nature with offensive war noises*

of authority

Rhyme change. Sound effect

context. *let your love die*

Trump . . . pibroch] battle-trumpet . . . bagpipe
the lark's shrill fife] i.e. instead of the wind-instrument that calls you to battle ('fife'), you will be
  woken by the equally high-pitched ('shrill') song of the lark

Karmic

Huntsman, rest! thy chase is done;
   While our slumbrous spells assail ye,
Dream not, with the rising sun,   *imposing,*
   Bugles here shall sound reveille. *yet benign*
- Sleep! the deer is in his den;
   - Sleep! thy hounds are by thee lying;
- Sleep! nor dream in yonder glen,
   How thy gallant steed lay dying.
Huntsman, rest! thy chase is done,
Think not of the rising sun,
For at dawning to assail ye,
Here no bugles sound reveille.

Extended metaphor
→ *this theme is death, slipping away*

131

The Dead Knight

JOHN MASEFIELD

The cleanly rush of the mountain air,
And the mumbling, grumbling humble-bees,
Are the only things that wander there,
The pitiful bones are laid at ease,
The grass has grown in his tangled hair,
And a rambling bramble binds his knees.

To shrieve his soul from the pangs of hell,
The only requiem-bells that rang
Were the hare-bell and the heather-bell.
Hushed he is with the holy spell
In the gentle hymn the wind sang,
And he lies quiet, and sleeps well.

He is bleached and blanched with the summer sun;
The misty rain and cold dew
Have altered him from the kingly one
(That his lady loved, and his men knew)
And dwindled him to a skeleton.

The vetches have twined about his bones,
The straggling ivy twists and creeps
In his eye-sockets; the nettle keeps
Vigil about him while he sleeps.
Over his body the wind moans
With a dreary tune throughout the day,
In a chorus wistful, eerie, thin
As the gull's cry—as the cry in the bay,
The mournful word the seas say
When tides are wandering out or in.

shrieve] absolve from sin   pangs] pains
requiem-bells] i.e. the bells rung at a Christian mass for the dead   vetches] wild plants

132

From the Coptic

STEVIE SMITH

Three angels came to the red red clay
Where in a heap it formless lay,

Stand up, stand up, thou lazy red clay,
Stand up and be Man this happy day.

Oh in its bones the red clay groaned,
And why should I do such a thing? it said,
And take such a thing on my downy head?
Then the first angel stood forth and said,

Thou shalt have happiness, thou shalt have pain,
And each shall fall turn and about again,
And no man shall say when the day shall fall
That thou shalt be happy or not at all.

And the second angel said much the same
While the red clay lay flat in the falling rain,
Crying, I will stay clay and take no blame.

Coptic] an old Egyptian language
red clay] i.e. the earth of which we are made (and the meaning of the name 'Adam', the first
   man in the Bible)

Then the third angel rose up and said,
Listen thou clay, raise thy downy head,
When thou hast heard what I have to say
Thou shalt rise Man and go man's way.

What have you to promise? the red clay moans,
What have you in store for my future bones?
I am Death, said the angel, and death is the end,
I am Man, cries clay rising, and you are my friend.

133

Futility

WILFRED OWEN

Move him into the sun –
Gently its touch awoke him once,
At home, whispering of fields unsown.
Always it woke him, even in France,
Until this morning and this snow.
If anything might rouse him now
The kind old sun will know.

Think how it wakes the seeds, –
Woke, once, the clays of a cold star.
Are limbs, so dear-achieved, are sides,
Full-nerved – still warm – too hard to stir?
Was it for this the clay grew tall?
– O what made fatuous sunbeams toil
To break earth's sleep at all?

the clays of a cold star] the earthly material that embodies our mysteriously distant spirit

134

The Pains of Sleep

SAMUEL TAYLOR COLERIDGE

Ere on my bed my limbs I lay,
It hath not been my use to pray
With moving lips or bended knees;
But silently, by slow degrees,
My spirit I to Love compose,
In humble trust mine eye-lids close,
With reverential resignation,
No wish conceived, no thought exprest,
Only a sense of supplication;
A sense o'er all my soul imprest
That I am weak, yet not unblest,
Since in me, round me, every where
Eternal Strength and Wisdom are.

But yester-night I prayed aloud
In anguish and in agony,
Up-starting from the fiendish crowd
Of shapes and thoughts that tortured me:
A lurid light, a trampling throng,
Sense of intolerable wrong,
And whom I scorned, those only strong!
Thirst of revenge, the powerless will
Still baffled, and yet burning still!

yester-night] last night, yesterday evening

Desire with loathing strangely mixed
On wild or hateful objects fixed.
Fantastic passions! maddening brawl!
And shame and terror over all!
Deeds to be hid which were not hid,
Which all confused I could not know
Whether I suffered, or I did:
For all seemed guilt, remorse or woe,
My own or others still the same
Life-stifling fear, soul-stifling shame.

So two nights passed: the night's dismay
Saddened and stunned the coming day.
Sleep, the wide blessing, seemed to me
Distemper's worst calamity.
The third night, when my own loud scream
Had waked me from the fiendish dream,
O'ercome with sufferings strange and wild,
I wept as I had been a child;
And having thus by tears subdued
My anguish to a milder mood,
Such punishments, I said, were due
To natures deepliest stained with sin, –
For aye entempesting anew
The unfathomable hell within,
The horror of their deeds to view,
To know and loathe, yet wish and do!
Such griefs with such men well agree,
But wherefore, wherefore fall on me?
To be beloved is all I need,
And whom I love, I love indeed.

Distemper's worst calamity] the very worst affliction to my disordered condition
aye entempesting anew] continually stirring up again
wherefore] why

135

[handwritten: ABBA ABBA ↳ Petrarchan sonnet]

I Dream of You...

CHRISTINA ROSSETTI *[handwritten: → Religious. Loved man of diff. religion, who's proposal she rejects + regrets]*

I dream of you, to wake: would that I might
    Dream of you and not wake but slumber on;
    Nor find with dreams the dear companion gone,
As, summer ended, summer birds take flight.
In happy dreams I hold you full in sight,
    I blush again who waking look so wan; *[handwritten: bridal]*
    Brighter than sunniest day that ever shone,
In happy dreams your smile makes day of night. *[handwritten: Bitter]* *[handwritten: Crystalises, Idealises, Preserves Him outside of reality]*
Thus only in a dream we are at one,
    Thus only in a dream we give and take
        The faith that maketh rich who take or give;
    If thus to sleep is sweeter than to wake, *[handwritten: Aye there's the rub]*
        To die were surely sweeter than to live,
Though there be nothing new beneath the sun.

[handwritten: In dreams same religion or neither]

[handwritten: Not questioning these religions cho[?] no 'rose by any other name'. More is belief in heaven.]

to wake] i.e. only then to wake up
wan] pale
nothing new beneath the sun] compare Ecclesiastes 1, 9: 'The thing that hath been, it is that which shall
  be; and that which is done is that which shall be done: and there is no new thing under the sun.'

136

Renouncement

ALICE MEYNELL

I must not think of thee; and, tired yet strong,
I shun the thought that lurks in all delight—
The thought of thee—and in the blue Heaven's height,
And in the sweetest passage of a song.
Oh, just beyond the fairest thoughts that throng
This breast, the thought of thee waits, hidden yet bright;
But it must never, never come in sight;
I must stop short of thee the whole day long.
But when sleep comes to close each difficult day,
When night gives pause to the long watch I keep,
And all my bonds I needs must loose apart,
Must doff my will as raiment laid away, —
With the first dream that comes with the first sleep
I run, I run, I am gathered to thy heart.

Renouncement] act of renunciation, relinquishment
needs must loose apart] have no choice but to untie
doff] remove, take off
as raiment laid away] as casually as a discarded garment

137

Nightsong: City

DENNIS BRUTUS

Sleep well, my love, sleep well:
the harbour lights glaze over restless docks,
police cars cockroach through the tunnel streets

from the shanties creaking iron-sheets
violence like a bug-infested rag is tossed
and fear is immanent as sound in the wind-swung bell;

the long day's anger pants from sand and rocks;
but for this breathing night at least,
my land, my love, sleep well.

cockroach] i.e. resemble black beetles as they scuttle
shanties] makeshift towns of the poor

138

Sleep

KENNETH SLESSOR

Do you give yourself to me utterly,
  Body and no-body, flesh and no-flesh,
Not as a fugitive, blindly or bitterly,
  But as a child might, with no other wish?
Yes, utterly.

Then I shall bear you down my estuary,
Carry you and ferry you to burial mysteriously,
Take you and receive you,
Consume you, engulf you,
In the huge cave, my belly, lave you
With huger waves continually.

And you shall cling and clamber there
And slumber there, in that dumb chamber,
Beat with my blood's beat, hear my heart move
Blindly in bones that ride above you,
Delve in my flesh, dissolved and bedded,
Through viewless valves embodied so –

Till daylight, the expulsion and awakening,
  The riving and the driving forth,
Life with remorseless forceps beckoning –
  Pangs and betrayal of harsh birth.

lave] wash
riving] (1) tearing off; (2) arrival
forceps] pincer-like instrument used to assist in birth

sleep → passive, end of suffering

Death

(139)

Care-charmer Sleep...

SAMUEL DANIEL

Sonnet form
~
develops argument

Care-charmer Sleep, son of the sable Night,
Brother to Death, in silent darkness born, *Sensory*
all of it? ← Relieve my languish, and restore the light,
With dark forgetting of my cares, return.
And let the day be time enough to mourn
The shipwreck of my ill-adventur'd youth; *regrets   loss of youth? or what happened*
Let waking eyes suffice to wail their scorn,
Without the torment of the night's untruth.
Cease, dreams, the images of day-desires,
To model forth the passions of the morrow:
Never let rising sun approve you liars,
To add more grief to aggravate my sorrow. *waking from dream aggravates*
        Still let me sleep, embracing clouds in vain,
Couplet   And never wake to feel the day's disdain. *Deathly yo*

Care-charmer] i.e. that which relaxes anxiety
sable] black
languish] melancholy idleness
ill-adventur'd] unluckily ventured
model forth] project
approve] i.e. prove you to be

140

To Sleep

SIR PHILIP SIDNEY

Come, Sleep, O Sleep, the certain knot of peace,
  The baiting-place of wit, the balm of woe,
The poor man's wealth, the prisoner's release,
  The indifferent judge between the high and low;
With shield of proof shield me from out the press
  Of those fierce darts Despair at me doth throw:
O make in me those civil wars to cease;
  I will good tribute pay, if thou do so.
Take thou of me smooth pillows, sweetest bed,
  A chamber deaf to noise and blind to light,
A rosy garland and a weary head;
    And if these things, as being thine by right,
      Move not thy heavy grace, thou shalt in me,
      Livelier than elsewhere, Stella's image see.

certain knot] sure security
baiting-place] resting place (by the side of a road)
indifferent] impartial
of proof] of tried and tested strength
from out the press] from the full shower
Stella's image] i.e. the image of the speaker's beloved

141

from *Paradise Lost*
('Evening in Paradise')

JOHN MILTON

[handwritten margin note: can even earn way back to god]

Now came still evening on, and twilight grey
Had in her sober livery all things clad;
Silence accompanied, for beast and bird,
They to their grassy couch, these to their nests
Were slunk, all but the wakeful nightingale;
She all night long her amorous descant sung;
Silence was pleased. Now glowed the firmament
With living sapphires; Hesperus that led
The starry host, rode brightest, till the moon
Rising in clouded majesty, at length
Apparent queen unveiled her peerless light,
And o'er the dark her silver mantle threw;
    When Adam thus to Eve: 'Fair consort, the hour
Of night, and all things now retired to rest,
Mind us of like repose; since God hath set
Labour and rest, as day and night to men
Successive, and the timely dew of sleep
Now falling with soft slumbrous weight inclines
Our eyelids; other creatures all day long
Rove idle, unemployed, and less need rest;
Man hath his daily work of body or mind
Appointed, which declares his dignity,
And the regard of Heaven on all his ways;
While other animals unactive range,
And of their doings God takes no account.

[handwritten margin note: anthropomorphism]

[handwritten margin note: Pastoral]

in her sober livery all things clad] i.e. clothed everything in her monochrome colours
descant] melodious song
firmament] sky
Hesperus] the evening star
Apparent] (1) evident; (2) heir-apparent
Mind us of] put us in mind of, prompt our thoughts to

Tomorrow ere fresh morning streak the east
With first approach of light, we must be risen,
And at our <u>pleasant labour</u>, to reform
Yon flowery arbours, yonder alleys green,
Our walks at noon, with branches overgrown,
That mock our scant manuring and require
More hands than ours to lop their wanton growth.
Those blossoms also, and those dropping gums,
That lie bestrewn unsightly and unsmooth,
Ask riddance, if we mean to tread with ease.....

Yon . . . yonder] those over there
scant manuring] limited cultivation
lop] prune
gums] resinous secretions

Red Dragon

142

Venus, Dusk Star

To the Evening Star

Beckons in the night

Nature, Personification

WILLIAM BLAKE → Romantic Poet
↳ nature, positives
↳ reals + imagined

Sonnet

maternal, feminin → gentle protection

Thou fair-haired angel of the evening,
Now, whilst the sun rests on the mountains, light
Thy bright torch of love; thy radiant crown
Put on, and smile upon our evening bed!
Smile on our loves; and, while thou drawest the
Blue curtains of the sky, scatter thy silver dew
On every flower that shuts its sweet eyes
In timely sleep. Let thy west wind sleep on
The lake; speak silence with thy glimmering eyes,
And wash the dusk with silver. Soon, full soon,
Dost thou withdraw; then the wolf rages wide,
And the lion glares through the dun forest.
The fleeces of our flocks are covered with
Thy sacred dew: protect them with thine influence.

Sun hands over to Venus, twilight

Fertility
→ dew
→ bed

Benevolent

mixed sensory

Sexual Interpretation
↓ Nature to Bless his Sex

Oberon blesses bridal bed

Midsummer Night's Dream
→ floral,
slip away,
→ nature

Rules Change,
↳ Chaos

Shakespeare

Tyga Tyga

→ Simplicity

Primitive urge romanticised

contrast

God Blood simple ↳ from wild animals (biblical)

violence

*ODE → Praise ↓
↓ eroticism*

Mankind → sheep
→ Plebs
→ impotence
→ Innocence
→ SIN of Man

Religious

Landscape

Prayerful

Anastrophe → inversion of typical word order
→ Brings attention to specific concepts
→ Poet's character

full soon] i.e. all too soon
dun] dark
sacred dew] i.e. the moon's silver light
thine influence] i.e. your astrological sway

Eden?

Caine + Abel?

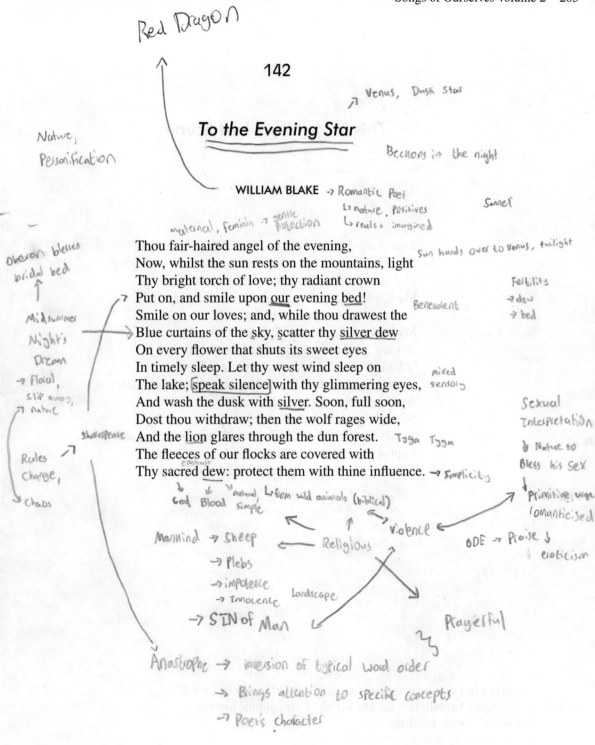

143

This is My Play's Last Scene

JOHN DONNE

This is my play's last scene, here heavens appoint
My pilgrimage's last mile; and my race
Idly, yet quickly run, hath this last pace,
My span's last inch, my minute's latest point,
And gluttonous death, will instantly unjoint
My body, and soul, and I shall sleep a space,
But my'ever-waking part shall see that face,
Whose fear already shakes my every joint:
Then, as my soul, to heaven her first seat, takes flight,
And earth-born body, in the earth shall dwell,
So, fall my sins, that all may have their right,
To where they are bred, and would press me, to hell.
Impute me righteous, thus purged of evil,
For thus I leave the world, the flesh, and devil.

my play's last scene] i.e. the final scene in the performance of my life
pilgrimage's last mile] i.e. the last stretch of my spiritual journey
unjoint] dislocate, break up
my'ever-waking part] i.e. my soul
first seat] primary destination
To where they are bred] i.e. to the earth, where sins are committed
press] (1) drag down; (2) forcibly enlist
Impute] judge

144

Upon the Image of Death

ROBERT SOUTHWELL

Before my face the picture hangs,
  That daily should put me in mind
Of those cold qualms and bitter pangs,
  That shortly I am like to find:
    But yet, alas, full little I
    Do think hereon that I must die.

I often look upon a face
  Most ugly, grisly, bare, and thin;
I often view the hollow place,
  Where eyes and nose had sometimes been;
    I see the bones across that lie,
    Yet little think that I must die.

I read the label underneath,
  That telleth me whereto I must;
I see the sentence eke that saith
  'Remember, man, that thou art dust!'
    But yet, alas, but seldom I
    Do think indeed that I must die.

Continually at my bed's head
  A hearse doth hang, which doth me tell,
That I ere morning may be dead,
  Though now I feel myself full well:
    But yet, alas, for all this, I
    Have little mind that I must die.

Image of Death] a picture of a skull, a memento mori
the bones across that lie] i.e. the cross-bones beneath a skull
sentence] caption, motto
eke] also

The gown which I do use to wear,
  The knife wherewith I cut my meat,
And eke that old and ancient chair
  Which is my only usual seat;
    All these do tell me I must die,
    And yet my life amend not I.

My ancestors are turned to clay,
  And many of my mates are gone;
My youngers daily drop away,
  And can I think to 'scape alone?
    No, no, I know that I must die,
    And yet my life amend not I.

Not Solomon, for all his wit,
  Nor Samson, though he were so strong,
No king nor person ever yet
  Could 'scape, but death laid him along:
    Wherefore I know that I must die,
    And yet my life amend not I.

Though all the East did quake to hear
  Of Alexander's dreadful name,
And all the West did likewise fear
  To hear of Julius Caesar's fame,
    Yet both by death in dust now lie.
    Who then can 'scape, but he must die?

If none can 'scape death's dreadful dart,
  If rich and poor his beck obey,
If strong, if wise, if all do smart,
  Then I to 'scape shall have no way.
    Oh! grant me grace, O God, that I
    My life may mend, sith I must die.

do use to wear] customarily wear
Solomon . . . Samson] i.e. the Biblical epitomes of wisdom and strength
Alexander's . . . Julius Caesar's] i.e. the epitomes of military glory in the ancient world
beck] beckoning gesture
sith] because, since

145

Death

WILLIAM BELL SCOTT

I am the one whose thought
Is as the deed; I have no brother, and
No father; years
Have never seen my power begin. A chain
Doth bind all things to me. In my hand, man,—
Infinite thinker,—vanishes as doth
The worm that he creates, as doth the moth
That it creates, as doth the limb minute
That stirs upon that moth. My being is
Inborn with all things, and
With all things doth expand.

But fear me not; I am
The hoary dust, the shut ear, the profound,
The deep of night,
When Nature's universal heart doth cease
To beat; communicating nothing; dark
And tongueless, negative of all things. Yet
Fear me not, man; I am the blood that flows
Within thee,—I am change; and it is I
Creates a joy within thee, when thou feel'st
Manhood and new untried superior powers
Rising before thee: I it is can make
Old things give place
To thy free race.

The worm that he creates] i.e. the worm (thought to be) engendered in his decomposing corpse
the limb minute] the tiny leg
free race] liberated generation

Not a negative, we ascribe no benevolence

All things are born <u>for me</u>.
His father and his mother,—yet man hates
    Me foolishly.
An easy spirit and a <u>free</u> lives on,
But he who fears the ice doth stumble. Walk
Straight onward peacefully,—I am a friend
Will pass thee graciously: but grudge and weep
And cark,—I'll be a <u>cold chain</u> round thy neck
Into the grave, each day a link drawn in,
Until thy face shall be upon the turf,
    And the hair from thy crown
    Be blown like thistle-down.

inherent
impasticity,
natural

Our power over death,
to accept its presence
in our lives

Voldemort - 'there is nothing
worse than
death'

cark] fret, worry, express undue anxiety
turf] the patch of earth of a grave
crown] head

146

Last Lines

'The following are the last lines my sister Emily ever wrote.'
(Charlotte Brontë)

EMILY BRONTË

No coward soul is mine,
No trembler in the world's storm-troubled sphere:
I see Heaven's glories shine,
And faith shines equal, arming me from fear.

O God within my breast,
Almighty, ever-present Deity!
Life—that in me has rest,
As I—undying Life—have power in thee!

Vain are the thousand creeds
That move men's hearts: unutterably vain;
Worthless as withered weeds,
Or idlest froth amid the boundless main,

To waken doubt in one
Holding so fast by thine infinity;
So surely anchored on
The steadfast rock of immortality.

Charlotte Brontë] (1816–1855), novelist, Emily's elder sister
creeds] beliefs
boundless main] endless ocean

from first 4 Stanzas

Shift

Escalates

Flatters

Humbling

With wide-embracing love
Thy spirit animates eternal years,   Old Testament
Pervades and broods above,
Changes, sustains, dissolves, creates, and rears.

to heaven

Man's
understanding →

insulting?
reconciling
new science
of size units?
w.
human miniscule
-ness

Though earth and man were gone,
And suns and universes ceased to be,
And thou were left alone,
Every existence would exist in thee.

There is not room for Death,   → Significant 2 ppl / not god
Nor atom that his might could render void:
Thou— thou art Being and Breath,   Matter
And what thou art may never be destroyed.

147

A Vision

JOHN CLARE

I lost the love, of heaven above;
I spurn'd the lust, of earth below;
I felt the sweets of fancied love,—
And hell itself my only foe.

I lost earth's joys, but felt the glow,
Of heaven's flame abound in me:
'Till loveliness, and I did grow,
The bard of immortality.

I loved, but woman fell away;
I hid me, from her faded fame:
I snatch'd the sun's eternal ray,—
And wrote 'till earth was but a name.

In every language upon earth,
On every shore, o'er every sea;
I gave my name immortal birth,
And kep't my spirit with the free.

spurn'd] rejected
fancied] imaginary

148

The Wizard's Funeral

RICHARD WATSON DIXON

For me, for me, two horses wait,
Two horses stand before my gate:
Their vast black plumes on high are cast,
Their black manes swing in the midnight blast,
Red sparkles from their eyes fly fast.
But can they drag the hearse behind,
Whose black plumes mystify the wind?
What a thing for this heap of bones and hair!
Despair, despair!
Yet think of half the world's winged shapes
Which have come to thee wondering:
At thee the terrible idiot gapes,
At thee the running devil japes,
And angles stoop to thee and sing
From the soft midnight that enwraps
Their limbs, so gently, sadly fair; –
Thou seest the stars shine through their hair.
I go to a mansion that shall outlast;
And the stoled priest that steps before
Shall turn and welcome me at the door.

black plumes] i.e. the black feathers worn by horses that pulled a hearse
japes] deceives, mocks
stoled] wearing priestly vestments

149

The Imprisoned Soul

WALT WHITMAN

At the last, tenderly,
From the walls of the powerful, fortress'd house,
From the clasp of the knitted locks—from the keep of the well-closed
   doors,
Let me be wafted.

Let me glide noiselessly forth;
With the key of softness unlock the locks—with a whisper
Set ope the doors, O soul!

Tenderly! be not impatient!
(Strong is your hold, O mortal flesh!
Strong is your hold, O love!)

keep] constraint; fortified tower

150

Requiem

ROBERT LOUIS STEVENSON

Under the wide and starry sky
Dig the grave and let me lie:
Glad did I live and gladly die,
  And I laid me down with a will.

This be the verse you grave for me:
Here he lies where he long'd to be;
Home is the sailor, home from sea,
  And the hunter home from the hill.

Requiem] the dirge sung for the repose of the dead
with a will] willingly
grave] engraved, inscribed

Index of First Lines